Abraham Lincoln's
DAILY TREASURE

Moments of Faith with America's Favorite President

EDITED BY THOMAS FREILING

D0188186

Revell

a division of Baker Publishing Group
Grand Rapids, Michigan

© 2002 by Thomas Freiling

Published by Revell
a division of Baker Publishing Group
P.O. Box 6287, Grand Rapids, MI 49516-6287
www.revellbooks.com

Paperback edition published 2014
ISBN 978-0-8007-2174-9

Printed in the United States of America
The Library of Congress has cataloged the previous edition as follows:
 Freiling, Tom.
     Abraham Lincoln's daily treasure : moments of faith with America's favorite
 president / Thomas Freiling.
       p. cm.
     ISBN-10: 0-8007-1809-7 (cloth)
     ISBN 978-0-8007-1809-1 (cloth)
       1. Lincoln, Abraham, 1809–1865—Religion. 2. Lincoln, Abraham, 1809–
 1865—Philosophy. 3. Lincoln, Abraham, 1809-1865—Quotations. 4. Conduct
 of life—Quotations, maxims, etc. 5. Christian life—Quotations, maxims, etc. 6.
 Presidents—United States—Biography. I. Title.
 E457.2 .F787 2002
 973.7'092—dc21   2002008572

Unless otherwise marked, Scripture is taken from the King James Version of the Bible.

Scripture marked RSV is taken from the Revised Standard Version of the Bible, copyright 1952 [2nd edition, 1971] by the Division of Christian Education of the National Council of the Churches of Christ in the United States of America. Used by permission. All rights reserved.

15   16   17   18   19   20   21   8   7   6   5   4

Acknowledgments

I want to thank the Abraham Lincoln Book Shop in Chicago for finding for me early twentieth-century, out-of-print books about Lincoln's religious views. The books of Edgar DeWitt, William J. Wolf, William Barton, and Dr. G. George Fox all provided invaluable research and resources.

I'm also grateful to Brian Peterson, acquisitions editor at Baker Book House, for allowing me the opportunity to share this treasure. Thanks also to Cheryl England, who dutifully transcribed notes and manuscripts. Finally, I want to thank my wife, Nancy, for her enduring support. She always helps the most.

Introduction

In this book I offer the reader daily doses of Abraham Lincoln's spiritual and moral axioms equaling a year's worth of godly advice from America's greatest president. I call them daily treasures, first, because many of them are based on a nineteenth-century devotional book used by Lincoln during the Civil War entitled *The Believer's Daily Treasure*. The second reason I call them treasures is because they will make you rich. Read them and you'll abound in godly wisdom and spiritual truth.

This book does not argue or contend. It does not build a case for or against what Lincoln believed about religion. Opinions based on evidence that seems to point in different directions vary widely and did even when he was alive. But this book does not weigh that evidence. That kind of scrutiny is best left to scholars and historians. I certainly have my own views, which I'll share with you. But my aim in this book is not to analyze. It is to inspire and motivate, to stir your soul with spiritual nuggets of the things Lincoln said and wrote about God, prayer, faith, and morality.

Lincoln's life was no easy road. He was poverty-stricken, self-taught, and for much of his life, a failure. He grieved the loss of his mother and two sons. He was homely and awkward. Yet he somehow got through it, rising above the depths of depression to become one of history's most venerable figures. From a lowly frontiersman to commander in chief and emancipator,

Lincoln grew in stature until the day of his death. Even today his image looms larger than life on the landscape of American history. If ever an American statesman reached a legendary, almost immortal status, it was Lincoln. Leo Tolstoy called him "a Christ in miniature."

This book gives you the proverbs of this great man, Abraham Lincoln, along with my own remarks and observations relating them to our lives today. This book will help you answer the question "What would Lincoln do?" Indeed, what Lincoln said 150 years ago does apply today. Like the Scripture itself, Lincoln's words are alive with the truth. They have a "perpetual freshness" and will live "as long as the conscience and memory of man," according to Lincoln archivist Archer Shaw.

If you're struggling to overcome the odds, if you've experienced great grief or loss in your life, or if it looks like you're about to lose a job or promotion, let Lincoln's words forge a way out. If you struggle to be honest, loyal, or humble, let Lincoln go to work on your character. If you give no time to God, struggle to find God's will. If you have no need of God's Word, let Lincoln stir your soul.

I discovered *The Believer's Daily Treasure* while browsing the dusty shelves of a used-book store. You see, I'm a rare book collector. While others spend their time on the golf course, I can be found at antiquarian book shops. I especially like to collect books about American history and government, probably because of my career in Washington, D.C., at the United States House of Representatives.

The small devotional, originally published in England in 1852, was filled with Scripture, prose, and poetry for every day of the year. This particular edition of *The Believer's Daily Treasure* contained notes written by Lincoln biographer Carl Sandburg.

Sandburg wrote that a well-worn copy of this pocket-size book, inscribed with Lincoln's own signature, had been discovered in an old library. Sandburg surmised that the long-lost book might indeed have been the pocket Bible Lincoln reportedly read from during the Civil War. Sandburg said that inside its pages Lincoln "could come upon many sentences and phrases famous, important and often quoted; and many of the passages in the book could have had special interest to him."

It was quite exciting to read the same devotions Lincoln may have used during his own personal prayer and meditation time. If Lincoln drew strength from it to overcome all sorts of obstacles, then I wanted some of that strength too! I found the devotions to be quite inspiring.

As I meditated with *The Believer's Daily Treasure,* I also began collecting my favorite Lincoln adages and combining them with reading from it. The combination of old-fashioned, Bible-based devotions and Lincoln's own spiritual words were, I thought, a real treasure. That's how this book was born.

I learned a lot about Lincoln as I edited this book, mostly about how much he relied on religious and spiritual principles to get by in life, to make important decisions, to comfort himself in sorrow, and to develop stronger character.

There is no doubt Abraham Lincoln wrote and said more about religion and spirituality than any other president in American history. From public podiums to private letters and conversations, Lincoln made it evident that he took the matter seriously. And while there is admittedly some conflicting evidence, I see no reason to believe Abraham Lincoln was anything but a Christian in the historical sense of the word.

In doing research for this book, I found that modern historians mostly avoid the topic. Maybe they don't want to admit what they know they'll find. While many books have been published about Lincoln, only a handful of them discuss his religious beliefs. There are books about his military prowess during the Civil War, his views on slavery, his oratorical skills, and his political ambitions. Hundreds of books focus on his tragic assassination, while others focus on his childhood and life as a young frontiersman. There are books filled with quotes and quips and others with stories. Some books look at Lincoln from the perspective of those who knew him best, while others are written from the perspective of Lincoln himself. There are books to help you apply Lincoln's management style in your small business, books about his relationships with women, and even one that reveals the secrets of his DNA code. But there are almost no books in print about Lincoln's faith in God. The best I could find was part of a book written by Marvin Olasky, senior fellow of The Acton Institute for the Study of Religion and Liberty. In his *The American Leadership Tradition,* Olasky looks at the Christian influences in Lincoln's life. But in compiling and editing this book, I had to look back more than half a century to find any complete books devoted to the subject.

Eventually I found what I was looking for. Early in the twentieth century, Lincoln's spiritual life was a subject of great public interest. In 1920 the prominent pastor and theologian William Barton wrote *The Soul of Lincoln.* Barton interviewed hundreds of those who knew Lincoln, and he collected thousands of letters, documents, and manuscripts about Lincoln's life. Barton's inquiry ultimately brought him to one conclusion: Abraham Lincoln believed and professed faith in the Christian God. He read the Bible, believed the New Testament message, and believed God both listened to and answered his prayers.

Soon afterward other books were written with similar conclusions. Dr. G. George Fox's *Abraham Lincoln's Religion* and William J. Wolf's *The Almost Chosen People: A Study of the Religion of Abraham Lincoln* both showed the importance of Lincoln's faith in God and his belief in Christianity. In his book *Lincoln and the Preachers,* Edgar DeWitt Jones went as far as to illustrate Lincoln's association with specific nineteenth-century churches and pastors. Jones recounts actual conversations Lincoln had with others about his Christian faith.

Many stories from Lincoln's life illustrate his religious convictions, but few stand out more than the story of September 22, 1862. It was on this day that Lincoln called a special meeting of his cabinet to announce the emancipation of slaves. Lincoln's announcement came as quite a surprise to the members of his cabinet. Years later several cabinet members penned their recollections of the meeting for the sake of posterity. Although there is some disagreement as to Lincoln's precise words, the diary of Secretary of the Navy Gideon Wells gives us the general idea of what Lincoln said. According to Wells, Lincoln told them "he had made a vow, a covenant, before God, that if He gave us victory over Lee in Pennsylvania, he would consider it his duty to move forward with the cause of emancipation." Wells said Lincoln expressed how much he was vexed over the decision, but he brought the matter before God, and "God had decided this question in favor of the slave."

I think that after you spend some time reflecting on the words in this book, you'll find every reason to believe Lincoln was a Christian according to the tenets of the historical Christian faith.

When Lincoln ran for Congress against the Reverend Peter Cartright, Lincoln was charged with being an "infidel" for not joining any particular Christian denomination. Cartright also suggested that Lincoln was a deist, or even worse, an atheist. Lincoln shrugged off the accusation, saying that he was never "a scoffer of Christianity" and that he "never denied the truth of the Scriptures." On the contrary, Lincoln embraced Judeo-Christian belief and the Bible.

There are no nuances to anything but orthodox Christianity in any of Lincoln's religious language. In fact, his idioms were often so biblical in nature he was once criticized for them. All his references to God, the Bible, and even Christ were grounded in the historical Christian faith. He used terms like "Almighty" and "the Heavenly Father" when he spoke or wrote about deity. He used the name of Jesus in both private and public conversation, and he was the only president to name the Holy Spirit in a proclamation.

It's true that Lincoln never applied for membership in any particular church or denomination, but that's not to say he didn't go to church. He was, in fact, a regular churchgoer. As a child he was raised in church, and after marrying Mary Todd he took a pew at the First Presbyterian Church of Springfield, where he dutifully attended for more than ten years. As president he was often seen strolling down the streets of Washington, D.C., visiting various churches on Sunday morning.

Historian Edgar DeWitt Jones painstakingly documented Lincoln's association with churches and pastors in his out-of-print book *Lincoln and the Preachers: How Lincoln Influenced the Life of Preachers and How the Preachers Influenced Lincoln.* Jones chronicled Lincoln's association with dozens of preachers and ministers, visits to churches, and hundreds of private conversations he had with clergy. William H. Townsend, author of *Lincoln the Litigant,* hailed the book as "unique in the annals of Lincolniana."

Not only did Lincoln attend church on a regular basis, he was also a student of the Bible. He put much of it to memory and referred to it specifically in public and private conversations. He alluded to stories from the Old Testament and to Jesus' words and parables. Lincoln colleague John Hanks once said of him, "He kept the Bible and Aesop's Fables always within reach and read them over and over again." Once Lincoln told his friend and colleague L. L. Chittenden, register of the treasury, "I decided a long time ago that it was less difficult to believe that the Bible was what it claimed to be than to disbelieve it."

Those who knew Lincoln best also remembered he was a man of prayer. He believed God heard his prayers, and he sought God's will through prayer. "I talk to God," Lincoln once told General Daniel Sickles, "because my mind is relieved when I do." He added, "When I could not see any other resort, I would place my whole reliance in God, knowing that all would go well, and that He would decide for the right."

This book shows how Lincoln believed in the Providence and sovereign will of God and looked to life eternal. Furthermore, it shows that he was God's instrument to be used for his purposes.

I hope you enjoy the daily treasures inside this book and that they will help you find your way through troubled times and help you to achieve greatness.

This Too Shall Pass Away

My times are in thy hand. . . . Make thy face to shine upon thy servant: save me for thy mercies' sake.

Psalm 31:15–16

> *"My times are in thy hand,"*
> *My God, I wish them there;*
> *My life, my friends, my soul, I leave*
> *Entirely to thy care.*

When Lincoln was defeated by rival Stephen A. Douglas for a seat in Congress, Lincoln's friends and colleagues showed much remorse. Not Lincoln. He encouraged his supporters, telling them to carry on without regret. In a letter he wrote to one supporter, Judge N. B. Judd, Lincoln said, "You are feeling badly, but this too shall pass away . . . never fear." Lincoln consoled his friends with a biblical paraphrase, telling them to persevere because all bad things eventually pass. That's good advice. If you're in the middle of a trial, remember that it will pass. There's nothing so bad that it can't be solved by time, especially in God's time.

It's Not Outward Appearances That Count

In this was manifested the love of God toward us, because that God sent his only begotten Son into the world, that we might live through him.

1 John 4:9

> *Pause, my soul, adore and wonder,*
> *Ask, Oh, why such love to me?*
> *Grace hath put me in the number*
> *Of the Saviour's family:*
> *Hallelujah!*
> *Thanks, eternal thanks to thee.*

Abraham Lincoln never was good at first impressions. One man who was present at one of Lincoln's famous addresses said, "When Lincoln rose to speak, I was greatly disappointed. He was so . . . angular and awkward that I had, for an instant, a feeling of pity for so ungainly a man." But after listening to Lincoln speak, this man's opinion changed. "Pretty soon," he said, "he began to get into his subject . . . [and] the whole man was transfigured. I forgot about his personal appearances. Forgetting myself, I was soon on my feet with the rest, yelling like a wild Indian, cheering this wonderful man. He's the greatest man since St. Paul!" Do you sometimes dismiss another person's views because of how he or she looks? Be careful not to put too much weight on outward appearances. You might just look past someone who could help you, become your best friend, or even help set you free.

On Greed

Whatsoever is born of God overcometh the world: and this is the victory that overcometh the world, even our faith.

1 John 5:4

> *'Tis faith that conquers earth and hell*
> *By a celestial power;*
> *This is the grace that shall prevail*
> *In the decisive hour.*

Mr. Roland Diller, who was one of Abraham Lincoln's neighbors in Springfield, Illinois, tells the following story: "I was called to the door one day by the cries of children in the street, and there was Mr. Lincoln, striding by with two of his boys, both of whom were wailing aloud. 'Why, Mr. Lincoln, what's the matter with the boys?' I asked. 'Just what's the matter with the whole world,' Lincoln replied. 'I've got three walnuts, and each wants two.'" Abraham Lincoln knew that most conflicts, however complex they might seem, really come down to one thing: greed. When we grow up, it's not walnuts we're concerned about. It's bigger houses, promotions, and new cars. But the principles are the same. When you focus on giving, not getting, you find yourself a much happier and more content person.

Keep Life Simple

He that is faithful in that which is least is faithful also in much: and he that is unjust in the least is unjust also in much.

Luke 16:10

Thy gifts are only then enjoy'd
When used as talents lent;
Those talents only well employ'd
When in his service spent.

Lincoln's habits in the Oval Office were as simple as they were at his home in Illinois. He never alluded to himself as "president" or as occupying "the presidency." "Call me Lincoln," he said to a friend. He grew weary of being called "Mr. President." He would even venture out of the White House, strolling down the streets of Washington, D.C., unprotected. Friends cautioned him about being so open in the midst of enemies, but he never heeded them. He liked to keep his life simple, unencumbered by "pomp and circumstance." Even when he joined the ranks of the rich and famous, he refused to change his lifestyle simply to make an impression. Abe Lincoln was still Abe Lincoln. If you feel pressured by others to act like someone you're not, take a stroll and remember that what is important is that you're happy with yourself.

Don't Settle for Mediocrity

If God so clothe the grass of the field, which to day is, and to morrow is cast into the oven, shall he not much more clothe you, O ye of little faith?

Matthew 6:30

I know not what may soon betide,
Or how my wants shall be supplied;
But Jesus knows, and will provide.

When creature comforts fade and die,
Worldlings may weep — but why should I?
Jesus still lives, and still is nigh.

As commander in chief, Lincoln expected the best in his generals. He would not countenance failure on the part of subordinates but doled out the severest punishment on those who did not win victories. After his defeat at Fredericksburg, Burnside was relieved by Hooker, who suffered defeat at Chancellorsville; Hooker was relieved by Meade, who won at Gettysburg but was refused promotion because he did not crush Lee. Then Rosecrans was all but defeated at Chickamauga and gave way to Grant, who of all the Union commanders never lost a battle. Grant was Lincoln's ideal leader, and he was never superseded. If you're looking for help, do you settle for less than average? Sometimes to win a war, you have to find the best and expect the best from those who are helping you.

Judge Not, Lest You Be Judged

The Lord said, Simon, Simon, behold, Satan hath desired to
have you, that he may sift you as wheat: But I have prayed for
thee, that thy faith fail not.

Luke 22:31–32

> *Though faint my prayers, and cold my love*
> *My stedfast hope shall not remove,*
> *While Jesus intercedes above.*
>
> *Against me earth and hell combine;*
> *But on my side is power Divine;*
> *Jesus is all, and he is mine.*

A United States senator who believed that every man who
believed in secession should be executed asked President Lincoln what he intended to do with Confederate soldiers after
the war was over. Lincoln said he planned to "forgive and forget," to reconstruct and unify the country. The senator proclaimed, "You are certainly crazy!" President Lincoln was
unmoved and patiently suggested that the senator accept the
post of chief executioner. "I am a gentleman, sir, and I certainly thought you knew me better than to believe me capable of doing such dirty work," said the senator as he left the
Oval Office, never to show his face there again. Lincoln was
quick to forgive, to have mercy on his friends in the South.
It would have been easy to judge them for their deeds, but
instead he was ready to grant them mercy to live in peace and
harmony. Are you a willing executioner, or are you like Lincoln, ready to forgive and forget?

Be Brave

Above all, taking the shield of faith, wherewith ye shall be able to quench all the fiery darts of the wicked.

Ephesians 6:16

Let faith exert its conquering power,
Say in thy tempted, trembling hour,
"My God, my Father, save thy son!"
'Tis heard—and all thy fears are done.

When Lincoln was a young soldier during the Black Hawk War, he showed what it means to be brave. An Indian came into the camp with a paper of safe conduct. But because the members of Lincoln's company were exasperated by recent Indian barbarities, they conspired to kill him. At the moment the men were about to shoot the Indian, Lincoln rushed forward, struck up the muskets with his hands, and standing in front of the victim, declared that he should not be killed. It was with great difficulty that the men could be kept from their purpose, but the courage and firmness of Lincoln thwarted them. Surely the men could have overpowered Lincoln, but the bravery of his convictions kept them from murdering the innocent Indian. The example of Lincoln's brave heart stopped the murder.

On Reputation

I love thy commandments above gold; yea, above fine gold. . . .
Thy testimonies are wonderful: therefore doth my soul keep
them.

Psalm 119:127, 129

> *Here mines of knowledge, love, and joy,*
> *Are open'd to our sight,*
> *The purest gold without alloy,*
> *And gems divinely bright.*

As Lincoln's legendary status arose across the country, some
proposed that in addition to being a great president, he was
also a military hero during the Black Hawk War. But Lincoln
refused to accept the accolades. He preferred that his reputation be founded on the truth, not on grandiose stories. Of his
experience during the war, Lincoln only acknowledged to have
had a "good many bloody struggles with the mosquitoes, and
although I never fainted from loss of blood, I can truly say
that I was often very hungry." If your friends started a rumor
that you were a military hero, would you accept your newfound reputation? Hopefully you'd do as Lincoln did and let
the truth be known. The reputation Lincoln gained as an honest man was much greater than if he had been remembered
as a brave soldier.

Be Cautious with Your Words

Search the scriptures; for in them ye think ye have eternal life: and they are they which testify of me.

John 5:39

Lord, thy teaching grace impart,
That we may not read in vain;
Write thy precepts on our heart,
Make thy truths and doctrine plain;
Let the message of thy love
Guide us to thy rest above.

    Superintendent Chandler of the Telegraph Office once told how President Lincoln wrote telegrams. "His method of composition was slow and laborious. It was evident that he thought out what he was going to say before he touched his pen to the paper. He would sit looking out of the window, his left elbow on the table, his hand scratching his temple, his lips moving, and frequently he spoke the sentence aloud or in a half whisper. After he was satisfied that he had the proper expression, he would write it out." Have you ever written a letter in haste, later regretting what you wrote? Like Lincoln, be cautious with your words, especially those you put on paper. It's hard to retract something you have written, as it has the appearance of permanence. When you communicate, think before you act.

On Making the Right Decisions

His delight is in the law of the LORD; and in his law doth he meditate day and night.

Psalm 1:2

I love in solitude to shed
The penitential tear;
And all his promises to plead,
When none but God is near.

I love to think on mercies past,
And future good implore;
And all my cares and sorrows cast
On him whom I adore.

Sometimes it's hard to make the right decision, especially if it might not be the popular decision in the eyes of other people. President Lincoln, however, made decisions based on what was right and what he knew to be true. In August 1864 he called for five hundred thousand more soldiers. The Union was depressed as the Confederates had, with a comparatively small force, almost beaten them. With election time nearing, many thought another call for men would injure, if not destroy, Lincoln's chances for reelection. A friend warned him, and Lincoln replied, "As to my reelection, it matters not. We must have the men. If I go down, I intend to go, like the *Cumberland,* with my colors flying!" If Lincoln had based his decision only on what other people might think, he would have lost both his reelection campaign and the war. Instead, he won both.

How to Win Over an Enemy

Thy words were found, and I did eat them; and thy word was unto me the joy and rejoicing of mine heart: for I am called by thy name, O LORD God of hosts.

Jeremiah 15:16

Oh may these heavenly pages be
My ever dear delight;
And still new beauties may I see,
And still increasing light.

Lincoln gives an example of how to best beat your enemy: make him your friend. The editor of the *New York Herald,* an influential and powerful man named James Gordon Bennett, was very critical of Lincoln as president and commander in chief and he wrote disparaging articles about him. This disturbed Lincoln. At the time, the *Herald* was as prominent as the *New York Times.* What did Lincoln do? He wrote Bennett a letter, offering him the position of French Mission.

Bennett declined the offer, but from that day until the day of the president's death, he was one of Lincoln's most appreciative friends and hearty supporters. Instead of taking revenge or retribution, Lincoln knew the way to best beat his enemy was to make him a friend.

On Acts of Kindness

Blessed is he that waiteth, and cometh to the thousand three hundred and five and thirty days. But go thou thy way till the end be: for thou shalt rest, and stand in thy lot at the end of the days.

Daniel 12:12–13

> *Jerusalem, my happy home,*
> *My soul still pants for thee;*
> *When shall my labours have an end*
> *In joy, and peace, and thee.*

One morning President Lincoln asked Major Eckert, on duty at the White House, "Who is that woman crying out in the hall? What is the matter with her?" Eckert said it was a woman who had been expecting to go down to the army to see her husband, but because an order recently had gone out prohibiting women from visiting the army, she could not see him. Mr. Lincoln sat moodily for a moment after hearing this story. Then suddenly his face lit up with pleasure. "Let's bring him up." The order was written, and the man was sent to Washington. It was spur-of-the-moment decisions like this, small acts of kindness, that endeared Lincoln to the American people. Do you take a break now and then to show an act of kindness? It will not only make you feel better, but it will help give you a reputation like Lincoln's.

How to Take Criticism

He that is slow to anger is better than the mighty; and he that ruleth his spirit than he that taketh a city.

Proverbs 16:32

Happy the man, whose cautious steps
Still keep the golden mean;
Whose life, by Scripture rules well form'd,
Declares a conscience clean.

With the possible exception of President Washington, Lincoln was the most criticized man who ever held public office in the United States. During the first half of his initial term, there was no epithet that was not applied to him. One newspaper in New York habitually characterized him as "that hideous baboon at the other end of the avenue" and declared that "Barnum should buy and exhibit him as a zoological curiosity." How would you take it if you were publicly ridiculed? Not many people are accustomed to it, and not many people could take it. But for Lincoln it mattered little. Why? Because he expected to be criticized. It didn't surprise him, and because he knew it came with the job, he didn't let it bother him. When you take on a big responsibility, you should expect to be criticized. Get ready for it, and then when it happens, it won't take you unawares.

How to Gain a Loyal Friend

Ye have need of patience, that, after ye have done the will of God, ye might receive the promise.

Hebrews 10:36

> *I would submit to all thy will,*
> *For thou art good and wise;*
> *Let every anxious thought be still,*
> *Nor one faint murmur rise.*
>
> *Thy love can cheer the darksome gloom,*
> *And bid me wait serene,*
> *Till hopes and joys immortal bloom*
> *And brighten all the scene.*

Abraham Lincoln once had to deliver a secret message to Governor Sam Houston of Texas. A conflict had arisen there between the Southern party and Governor Houston. President Lincoln heard about the trouble and decided to try to get a message to the governor, offering United States support if he would put himself at the head of the state's Union party. Lincoln told the messenger, "This is a secret message. No one besides my cabinet knows anything about it, and we all are sworn to secrecy. Raise your right hand, and I am going to swear you in as one of my cabinet." The man, G. H. Giddings, became an official member of Lincoln's cabinet that day, and he immediately delivered the message. Lincoln knew the best way to secure Giddings's loyalty was to express confidence in him. Giddings felt proud that Lincoln would put so much trust in him. That's how to gain a loyal friend.

When to Resign

The trying of your faith worketh patience. But let patience have her perfect work, that ye may be perfect and entire, wanting nothing.

James 1:3–4

Through waves, and clouds, and storms,
He gently clears thy way:
Wait thou his time — the darkest night
Shall end in brightest day.

Here's a lesson about quitting. A few days before Lincoln's death, Stanton tendered his resignation as secretary of war. He accompanied the act with a heartfelt tribute to Lincoln's friendship and devotion to the country. He said he had accepted the position to hold it only until the war should end, and now that his work was done, it was his duty to resign. President Lincoln was greatly moved by Stanton's words. Throwing his arms around him, he said, "Stanton, you have been a good friend and a faithful public servant, and it is not for you to say when you will no longer be needed here." If you find a trusted friend or colleague who wants to quit, let that person know how important he or she is to you and that you simply won't accept the resignation. You might find that your friend or colleague didn't think he or she was wanted anymore. All that person needed was your continued confidence.

Make the Best of It

Because thou hast kept the word of my patience, I also will keep thee from the hour of temptation.

Revelation 3:10

Thus preserved from Satan's wiles,
Safe from dangers, free from fears,
May I live upon thy smiles,
Till the promised hour appears:
When the sons of God shall prove
All their Father's boundless love.

Before young Abraham Lincoln became an attorney, he accepted a clerical job at the local post office, eventually becoming its postmaster, because nobody else wanted the tedious, mind-numbing work. If the work was so boring, why did Abraham Lincoln aspire to be a mailman? He later told a friend it was because it gave him the opportunity to read every newspaper in the vicinity, helping him to learn more about his community and the country. Because Lincoln was poor, he had never been able to get half the newspapers he wanted before. This supposed menial job turned out to be quite an education for Lincoln and one that helped propel him into local politics. Sometimes in life you have to look a little harder to make the best of your situation. You can learn something from just about anything. Like Lincoln, even if you're unhappy with your present state, you should try to make the best of it. You might be surprised at how much you learn.

Acts of Mercy

We then that are strong ought to bear the infirmities of the weak, and not to please ourselves.

Romans 15:1

When weaker Christians we despise,
We do the great Redeemer wrong;
For God, the gracious and the wise,
Receives the feeble with the strong.

Secretary of State Leonard Swett once told a story about Abraham Lincoln's sympathetic and caring personality. "I remember one day being in his room when Lincoln was sitting at his table with a large pile of papers before him, and after a pleasant talk he turned quite abruptly and said: 'Get out of the way, Swett; tomorrow is butcher-day, and I must go through these papers and see if I cannot find some excuse to let these poor fellows off.'" The pile of papers he had were the records of court martials of men who on the following day were to be shot. Instead of doing the easy thing—just signing the papers—Lincoln was prepared to sift through each one, to find ways to save the lives of as many as possible. Do you work at being merciful, or is it something that just happens every once in a while? Lincoln worked at it, because he knew if he didn't, nobody else would.

On Humility

Remember them that are in bonds, as bound with them; and them which suffer adversity, as being yourselves also in the body.

Hebrews 13:3

With pity let my breast o'erflow,
When I behold another's woe;
And bear a sympathizing part,
Whene'er I meet a wounded heart.

Judge Joseph Gillespie was a friend of Abraham Lincoln and went to Springfield to see him shortly before Lincoln's departure for the presidential inauguration. "It was," said Judge Gillespie, "Lincoln's Gethsemane. He feared he was not the man for the great position and the great events that confronted him. Untried in national affairs, unversed in international diplomacy, unacquainted with the men who were foremost in the politics of the nation, he groaned when he saw the inevitable War of the Rebellion coming on. It was in humility of spirit that he told me he believed that the American people had made a mistake in selecting him." It is almost unbelievable that a man as capable as Lincoln would feel so inadequate. It is a testament to his humility and his ability to see the hugeness of the task at hand. While many other politicians would have jumped at the chance to be president, Lincoln knew the hugeness of the task was bigger than any one man. The next time you're looking for someone to help you with a big task, try those who tell you they're not so sure they can help.

Know God

As we have therefore opportunity, let us do good unto all men, especially unto them who are of the household of faith.

Galatians 6:10

Awake, my charity, and feed
The hungry soul, and clothe the poor;
In heaven are found no sons of need,
There all these duties are no more.

Despite a lifetime of trials and tribulations, Lincoln's disposition was remarkably content. Even during the darkest days of the Civil War, he portrayed a peace that surpassed the nation's understanding. "It is difficult to make a man miserable," he said, "when he feels worthy of himself and claims kindred to the great God who made him." Do you have a relationship with God that helps you look past your present circumstances? President Lincoln's self-assurance came, not from self-reliance, but from his knowledge of God.

Be Hopeful

Brethren, if a man be overtaken in a fault, ye which are spiritual, restore such an one in the spirit of meekness; considering thyself, lest thou also be tempted.

Galatians 6:1

Lord, we would strive, and hope, and wait,
The offending still to reinstate;
And when a broken heart we view,
Our Christian friendship quick renew.

Lincoln always looked forward to the promise of a better tomorrow, even in the face of his troubling circumstances. "The power of hope upon the human exertion and happiness is wonderful," he once remarked. It was Lincoln's hopefulness that heartened the Union through the Civil War. Rather than dwelling on the past or the present, Lincoln helped the country focus on the future. Are you hopeful for the future, or are you stuck in the past? Like Lincoln, you can develop an optimism based on hope for the future.

Hold No Resentment

Pure religion and undefiled before God and the Father is this, To visit the fatherless and widows in their affliction, and to keep himself unspotted from the world.

James 1:27

The poor are always with us here:
'Tis our great Father's plan,
That mutual wants and mutual care
Should bind us man to man.

President Lincoln wanted desperately to defeat the Confederacy, but at the same time, he didn't hold feelings of resentment against his enemy. His will to defeat them was tempered by his will to find peace and to dwell with them once again in unity. "We reinstate the spirit of concession and compromise," he said near the war's end. "It's the spirit which has never failed us in past perils, and which may be safely trusted for all the future." Do you hold hard feelings toward those who have hurt you in the past? If you're at war with other people or things, be prepared to forgive and forget. Like Lincoln, you can trust the spirit of compromise.

Seek God's Will

I will bless the LORD, who hath given me counsel: my reins also instruct me in the night seasons.

Psalm 16:7

Sure the Lord thus far has brought me,
By his watchful tender care;
Sure, 'tis he himself has taught me
How to seek his face by prayer:
After so much mercy past,
Will he give me up at last?

Seeking God's will can be frustrating. It certainly was for Lincoln. "There is no contending against the will of God," he said, "but still there is some difficulty in ascertaining, and applying it, to particular cases." When Lincoln was confronted by unusual circumstances, trials, or tribulations, he sought harder to understand what God was doing and why. Are you seeking God's will for your life, or are you confused and frustrated by your circumstances? God does have a purpose for your life, and he wants you to diligently seek it out.

Do God's Will

Know ye not that ye are the temple of God, and that the Spirit of God dwelleth in you?

1 Corinthians 3:16

Think what Spirit dwells within thee;
Think what Father's smiles are thine;
Think that Jesus died to win thee:
Child of heaven, canst thou repine?

Once God tells you to do something, it's important not to give up, no matter how much resistance you come up against. When Lincoln was criticized for emancipating the slaves, he proclaimed, "Whatever shall appear to be God's will I will do!" Lincoln stood his ground, never letting his detractors change his mind. His diligent pursuit of God's will ultimately led to national unity and freedom. Have you given up on God's call for your life? Make your own proclamation, and when other people tell you it won't work, be obstinate and tell them you will do it!

Promote Reconciliation

The Spirit also helpeth our infirmities: for we know not what we should pray for as we ought: but the Spirit itself maketh intercession for us with groanings which cannot be uttered.

Romans 8:26

> *Let pure devotion's fervours rise,*
> *Let every holy feeling glow;*
> *Oh, let the rapture of the skies*
> *Kindle in our cold hearts below.*
> *Come, vivifying Spirit, come,*
> *And make our hearts thy constant home.*

"Persuade your neighbor to compromise whenever you can," the young Abe Lincoln counseled a law student. It was unusual advice coming from a lawyer, someone whose profession involved being adversarial. But Lincoln preferred not to take sides. Instead, he helped other people settle their differences. He was a reconciler. It was for this reason people liked to confide in Lincoln and ask him for advice. Are you a peacekeeper or a troublemaker? The next time an argument flares up in your face, try not to pick a side, but be a reconciler and help to settle differences.

There's Never Enough to Argue

This is the confidence that we have in him, that, if we ask any thing according to his will, he heareth us.

1 John 5:14

He who for man their Surety stood,
And poured on earth his precious blood,
Pursues in heaven his mighty plan,
The Saviour and the friend of man.

With boldness, therefore, at the throne,
Let us make all our sorrows known;
And ask the aid of heavenly power,
To help us in the evil hour.

Abraham Lincoln was a man of action. While others squabbled and bickered, he made things happen. Instead of participating in fruitless, endless arguments, he spent his time and energy making a positive difference in the lives of other people. "A man has no time to spend half his life in quarrels," wrote Lincoln. Are you apt to pick a fight when you could be taking action? It's easy to get off-course in life with endless wrangling. Instead of trying to win arguments, you could better spend your passions and energy on things that matter. Be like Lincoln—don't quarrel. Make up your mind to stay focused on important things.

Stay Focused

Thou, when thou prayest, enter into thy closet, and when thou hast shut thy door, pray to thy Father which is in secret; and thy Father which seeth in secret shall reward thee openly.

Matthew 6:6

> *Far from the paths of men, to Thee*
> *I solemnly retire;*
> *See Thou, who dost in secret see,*
> *And grant my heart's desire.*

One of Lincoln's greatest strengths was his ability to keep his attention on the primary things. It's easy to get sidelined in life. The hectic pace often dissuades us from the important things. "At every step we must be true to the main purpose," Lincoln reminded the country during the Civil War. For Lincoln, the main purpose of the Union was justice, freedom, and unity. He stayed focused and kept moving toward it. Are you attentive to the main purpose of your life, or are you off-focus? Think about the things that are most important to you and try to stay true to your main purpose.

Be a Good Friend

Even them will I bring to my holy mountain, and make them joyful in my house of prayer.

Isaiah 56:7

Prayer makes the darken'd cloud withdraw,
Prayer climbs the ladder Jacob saw;
Gives exercise to faith and love,
Brings every blessing from above.

The absence of enemies doesn't amount to much if you don't have any friends. Abraham Lincoln valued friendship, and while other people concentrated on winning at all costs, Lincoln refused to let his will to win ruin his relationships. "Even the loss of enemies does not compensate for the loss of friends," he reminded his cabinet during the Civil War. Lincoln worked hard to find ways to maintain friends by spending time with them and communicating with them in letters. Do you work at your friendships? Maintaining them takes time and energy, but the results—having others who will stand by you and support you—are worthwhile.

Sincerity Persuades

Watch and pray, that ye enter not into temptation.

Matthew 26:41

> *Go to dark Gethsemane,*
> *Ye that feel the tempter's power,*
> *Your Redeemer's conflict see,*
> *Watch with him one bitter hour;*
> *Turn not from his griefs away,*
> *Learn of Jesus Christ to pray.*

While other people might try to persuade with eloquent speech or with logical arguments, Lincoln knew the best way to influence people was through the heart. "If you would win a man to your cause, first convince him that you are his sincere friend," he recommended to a colleague. "Therein is a drop of honey that catches his heart, which . . . when once gained, you will find but little trouble in convincing his judgment of the justice of your cause." How do *you* win friends and influence people? If you can't seem to get people on board with you, maybe it's because they don't feel like you care about them. Try tugging on their hearts, and soon their minds will follow. Lincoln cared about other people. In turn, the country cared about him.

Deserters Always Lose

This one thing I do, forgetting those things which are behind, and reaching forth unto those things which are before, I press toward the mark for the prize of the high calling of God in Christ Jesus.

Philippians 3:13–14

A scrip on my back, and a staff in my hand,
I march on in haste through an enemy's land:
The road may be rough, but it cannot be long,
So I'll smooth it with hope, and I'll cheer it with song.

One of Lincoln's biggest challenges as commander in chief was to keep his troops from quitting. The horrors of battle caused many soldiers to run away. So he set an example. He told them, "Many free countries have lost their liberty, and ours may lose hers; but if she shall, be it my proudest plume, not that I was the last to desert, but that I never deserted her." Lincoln let all those around him know that he'd be there at the end. Are you committed to be available to your family and friends always? Make a vow that you will always be there, that you won't ever desert them. If you keep your vow, you'll never lack the support to achieve your life's goals.

Don't Take It Personally

Let us not be weary in well doing: for in due season we shall reap, if we faint not.

Galatians 6:9

> *Meek pilgrim Zionward, if thou*
> *Hast put thy hand unto the plough,*
> *Oh look not back, nor droop dismay'd,*
> *At thought of victory delay'd:*
> *Doubt not that thou, in season due,*
> *Shall own his gracious promise true;*
> *And thou shalt share their glorious lot,*
> *Whom doing well hath wearied not.*

Self-deprecation can be painful, but Lincoln knew it strengthened his position in the hearts and minds of other people. "I feel like I once did when I met a woman riding horseback in the woods," he once quipped. "As I stopped to let her pass, she also stopped and, looking at me, said, 'I do believe you are the ugliest man I ever saw.' Said I, 'Madam, you are probably right, but I can't help it!' 'No,' said she, 'you can't help it, but you might stay at home!'" When is the last time you poked fun at yourself? If you take yourself too seriously, others will too. If you let your guard down once in a while, it will give others the chance to be transparent with you. Nobody is perfect, and it will help you feel better about yourself if you simply let everyone know up front that you are going to make mistakes.

Talk to God

Take unto you the whole armour of God, that ye may be able to withstand in the evil day, and having done all, to stand.

Ephesians 6:13

> *The Christian warrior—see him stand*
> *In the whole armour of his God;*
> *The Spirit's sword is in his hand,*
> *His feet are with the gospel shod.*

People often would come to President Lincoln for advice. One day General Sickles asked him for help about a particular matter relating to the war. Lincoln didn't have the answer, but he told the general where to look for it. "I am a full believer that God knows what he wants men to do—that which pleases him," he said. "It is never well with the man who heeds it not. I talk to God. My mind is relieved when I do." Where do you go for help? When Lincoln couldn't find an answer to a problem, he prayed to God for the answer. If you go to other people for help, you'll probably end up with a lot of different answers and none that you can trust completely. Take Lincoln's advice: Go to God for help. You can trust his answer.

Give God Credit

That on the good ground are they, which in honest and good heart, having heard the word, keep it, and bring forth fruit with patience.

Luke 8:15

Father of mercies, we have need
Of thy preparing grace;
Let the same hand that gives the seed
Provide a fruitful place.

Lincoln's close friend Joshua Speed got married as a result of an introduction Lincoln made at a ball. When Joshua thanked the president many years later, Lincoln refused to take the credit. "I believe God made me one of the instruments of bringing your family and you together, which union, I have no doubt, he foreordained." Lincoln was humble enough to know that the sovereignty of God was undeniable. Do you give God enough credit? We sometimes take the credit for something that was really beyond our control. The next time someone thanks you, try turning the thanks over to God, who makes all things possible. You'll be surprised at how others respond to your modest reply.

The Problem with Advice

That ye may walk honestly toward them that are without, and that ye may have lack of nothing.

1 Thessalonians 4:12

> *Come, let us search our ways, and try*
> *Have they been just and right;*
> *Is the great rule of equity*
> *Our practice and delight?*
>
> *In all we sell, in all we buy,*
> *Is justice our design?*
> *Do we remember God is nigh,*
> *And fear the wrath Divine?*

In a conversation with L. E. Chittenden, Registrar of the Treasury, Lincoln once explained why, at times, he ignored the advice of other people. "In almost every instance where I have yielded to the views of others, I have had occasion to regret it," he told Chittenden. "I am satisfied that when the Almighty wants me to do or not to do a particular thing, he finds a way of letting me know." Lincoln knew better than to rely on human advice. Instead, he went to God for answers. Do you rely on earthly advice or on heavenly answers? Don't rely too much on the opinions of other people when God is able and willing to give you the answers through prayer.

Be God's Instrument

If the Son therefore shall make you free, ye shall be free indeed.

John 8:36

Sweet is the freedom Christ bestows,
With which he makes his people free,
A liberty no mortal knows
Till thy his great salvation see.

A slave in North Carolina once exclaimed to Colonel Jim McKaye of New York, "Lincoln is everywhere. He knows everything and walks the earth like the Lord!" When Colonel McKaye conveyed the story to President Lincoln, Lincoln responded, "It is a momentous thing to be the instrument, under God, of the liberation of a race." Lincoln recognized that he was God's instrument, to be used for his purposes. Are you God's instrument, or do you run your life according to your own rules? From Lincoln's perspective, God's hand was directing the country. He was only God's humble instrument in the task. Think of yourself as a vessel God created for his purposes. Let God use you and your gifts for his glory.

Be Selfless

Stand fast therefore in the liberty wherewith Christ hath made us free, and be not entangled again with the yoke of bondage.

Galatians 5:1

> *From Egypt lately freed*
> *By the Redeemer's grace,*
> *A rough and thorny path we tread*
> *In hopes to see his face.*
>
> *The flesh dislikes the way,*
> *But faith approves it well;*
> *This only leads to endless day,*
> *All others lead to hell.*

Before Abraham Lincoln met his wife, Mary Todd, he made his intentions clear that whomever he might marry, he would make her happy. He once told a friend, "Whatever woman may cast her lot with mine, should any ever do so, it is my intention to do all in my power to make her happy and contented; and there is nothing I can imagine that would make me more unhappy than to fail in the effort." Lincoln's selfless approach to life was uncommon and an example for us all. Is your aim in life to make yourself happy or to make other people happy? If you, like Lincoln, set as your goal in life to make other people happy, the end result will very likely be that you too will be happy.

Be Selfless

All things whatsoever ye would that men should do to you,
do ye even so to them: for this is the law and the prophets.

Matthew 7:12

> *Blessed Redeemer, how divine,*
> *How righteous is this rule of thine,*
> *To do to all men just the same*
> *As we expect or wish from them.*
>
> *How bless'd would every nation prove*
> *Thus ruled by equity and love!*
> *All would be friends without a foe*
> *And form a paradise below.*

Even before Lincoln was assassinated, his image loomed
large. His legendary status caused all sorts of rumors and stories to abound. But he refused to let his pride swell. Once when
praised for his actions as president, he responded to the compliment with a reprimand. "I have never done an official act,"
he said sternly, "with a view to promote my personal aggrandizement, and I don't like to begin now." Unlike many leaders, Lincoln didn't have to promote himself in the eyes of other
people. He knew honesty was self-promoting. Do you seek
attention? Do you brag about your accomplishments? Lincoln
learned that to be an honest and unselfish person was usually
all that was necessary to gain the respect of other people.

Never Say Never

Keep yourselves in the love of God, looking for the mercy of our Lord Jesus Christ unto eternal life.

Jude 21

Rejoice in glorious hope;
Jesus, the Judge, shall come,
And take his servants up
To their eternal home.
Lift up your heart, lift up your voice;
Rejoice, he bids his saints rejoice.

As a young man, Lincoln's heart was crushed by the death of his fiancée. At the time, he made one promise he couldn't keep. "I have now come to the conclusion never again to think of marrying. For this reason, I can never be satisfied with anyone who would be blockhead enough to have me." Lincoln did, of course, marry. He learned to never say never to love. Have you given up on love, or do you have the faith that God will provide a lifelong partner for you? It may seem like God has given up on you, like you'll never feel like loving again. Remember Abraham Lincoln, who found the love he thought he'd never feel again.

Never Doubt God's Timing

I can do all things through Christ which strengtheneth me.

Philippians 4:13

I can do all things, and can bear
All sufferings, if my Lord be near;
Sweet pleasures mingle with the pains,
While his left hand my head sustains.

Even when you have faith in God, it's not easy to have faith in God's timing. We want God to answer our prayers—now. Lincoln understood how badly the country wanted God to answer its prayer to end the war—quickly. But in quiet desperation, he begged citizens, "Let us be quite sober. Let us diligently apply the means, never doubting that a just God, in his own good time, will give us the rightful result." Is your faith in God big enough to trust his timing? It may seem like an eternity to you, but because God looks at things from an eternal perspective, you can trust he knows the best time to answer your prayers.

Learn from Your Mistakes

We know that all things work together for good to them that love God, to them who are the called according to his purpose.

Romans 8:28

God will keep his own anointed;
Naught shall harm them, none condemn;
All their trials are appointed;
All must work for good to them:
All shall help them
To their heavenly diadem.

When Lincoln was elected president, he humbly gave the reason why he knew he'd be a success. "I am very sure that if I do not go away from here a wiser man," he said, "I shall go away a better man, for having learned here what a very poor sort of man I am." Winning the race isn't always what is most important. Understanding why you lost may be just the victory you need. Lincoln learned the real secret to success in life was to learn from mistakes. Have you let failure get you down, or is failure your teacher? Nobody can go through life succeeding all the time. But most people give up too early. Take Lincoln's view of success and failure. If you fail, you've learned something to help you succeed.

Make People Laugh

By whom [Jesus Christ] also we have access by faith into this grace wherein we stand, and rejoice in hope of the glory of God.

Romans 5:2

By faith to Pisgah's top I fly,
And there delighted stand,
To view beneath a cloudless sky,
The spacious promised land.

The Lord of all the vast domain
Has promised it to me;
The length and breadth of all the plain,
As far as faith can see.

Lincoln was known for his humor. It's ironic that someone who experienced so much pain and grief could be so funny. "Laughter [is] the joyous, beautiful, universal evergreen of life," he said. Lincoln was so well known for his comedic mannerisms, friends would seek him out just to hear a new story or witty quip. Being around Abraham Lincoln made people feel better. He had just the right medicine for a country in pain. Do you have fun in life? Do other people think it's fun to be around you? Lincoln was never lonely for friends, because other people always wanted to be with him. Try poking some fun and see how many new friends you find.

Help Others Grow

We glory in tribulations: also knowing that tribulation worketh patience; and patience, experience; and experience, hope.

Romans 5:3–4

Then let us wait the' appointed day,
Nor call this world our home;
To pilgrims in a foreign land,
Afflictions needs must come.

Who rules the world, o'errules their end,
They destined are for good;
And bear the saints to realms of rest,
Though mighty as a flood.

Helping other people grow—mentally, physically, and spiritually—was one of Lincoln's aims in life. He liked to see
people do better for themselves. "We proposed to give all a
chance. And we expect the weak to grow stronger, the ignorant, wiser; and all better and happier together," he told a
crowd during a campaign stop. Wherever Lincoln went, he
stirred people to improve themselves and their surroundings.
Do you help others grow? Helping other people grow is the
real way to find personal growth and development. Lincoln's
abilities to lead grew when he was given the opportunity to
help the nation grow. You can do the same.

Have Fun While You're at It

Why art thou cast down, O my soul? and why art thou disquieted in me? hope thou in God: for I shall yet praise him for the help of his countenance.

Psalm 42:5

The gloomiest day hath gleams of light,
The darkest wave hath bright foam near it;
And twinkles through the cloudiest night
Some solitary star to cheer it.

Are the gregarious less successful in life? Lincoln didn't think so. And if they were, then he didn't want any part of success. "It's a common notion that those who laugh heartily often never amount to much. . . . If this be the case, farewell to all my glory," he insisted. If you can't enjoy life, with all its pleasures, and still be successful, then Lincoln thought it was probably better to just enjoy life. Have the pressures of your life made things dry and dull? Has success been "worth it" for you? If not, then check to see if you're still able to enjoy yourself in the midst of success. Lincoln did. So can you.

Choose Your Words Wisely

When the Comforter is come, whom I will send unto you from the Father, even the Spirit of truth, which proceedeth from the Father, he shall testify of me.

John 15:26

In the hour of my distress,
When temptations me oppress,
And when I my sins confess —
Sweet Spirit, comfort me.

Those who talk the most often say the least. That was Lincoln's philosophy. Even before he was elected president, Abraham Lincoln was known for his quiet, reflective manner. He preferred listening to speaking, and when he did speak, it mattered. "I am very little inclined on any occasion to say anything," he admitted, "unless I hope to produce some good by it." Do you talk too much, spending time in endless chatter? Often those who say the least seem the wisest. Be careful what you say and how you say it. Think before you speak. Then you, like Lincoln, will be recognized by others to be wise.

Let God Be Sovereign

Now our Lord Jesus Christ himself, and God, even our Father, which hath loved us, and hath given us everlasting consolation and good hope through grace.

2 Thessalonians 2:16

In every trouble, sharp and strong,
My soul to Jesus flies;
My anchor-hold is firm on him,
When swelling billows rise.

After several years of war, Lincoln felt helpless. "I attempt no compliment to my own sagacity. I claim not to have controlled events, but confess plainly that events have controlled me," he admitted. "Now, at the end of three years' struggle, the nation's condition is not what any man devised or expected. God alone can claim it." Instead of despairing in his own lack of success, he acknowledged that God was in control. All that was left for Lincoln to do was to give it up to God. Have you given God your hopeless situations? Instead of despairing, tell God that you're giving your troubles up to him.

Don't Run with the Crowd

Although the fig tree shall not blossom, neither shall fruit be in the vines; the labour of the olive shall fail, and the fields shall yield no meat; the flock shall be cut off from the fold, and there shall be no herd in the stalls: Yet I will rejoice in the LORD, I will joy in the God of my salvation.

Habakkuk 3:17–18

Although my wealth and comfort's lost,
My blooming hopes cut off I see,
Yet will I in my Saviour trust,
Whose matchless grace can reach to me.

Lead or be led. That's the issue Abraham Lincoln often faced during the country's crisis. During the war, there was a lot of talk about quitting. He urged his fellow Americans not to yield to popular whims and trendy thinking, but to be strong in God's sovereignty. "Let there be no compromise on the question of extending slavery," he said. "If there be, all our labor is lost, and ere long, must be done again. The dangerous ground is Popular Sovereignty. Have none of it. Stand firm." Does peer pressure dictate what you believe? Don't let other people change your mind just because things don't appear to be going the way they ought. Be diligent.

Ignore Your Critics

This is my comfort in my affliction: for thy word hath quickened me.

Psalm 119:50

> *Thus trusting in thy word, I tread*
>   *The narrow path of duty on;*
> *What though some cherish'd joys are fled?*
>   *What though some flattering dreams are gone?*
> *Yet purer, brighter joys remain:*
> *Why should my spirit then complain?*

President Lincoln often refused to read the newspaper. He didn't want to know what others were saying about him but instead stayed focused on what he felt called to do. "If I were to try to read, much less answer, all the attacks made on me, this shop might as well be closed for any other business," he confided to a friend. "I do the very best I know how—the very best I can; and I mean to keep doing so until the end." Do you open yourself up to criticism? Do you listen too much to what other people are saying about you? Don't take so much credence in other people's opinions. Lincoln didn't. He stayed true to what he knew was right.

Become a Living Witness

Let all those that put their trust in thee rejoice: let them ever shout for joy, because thou defendest them: let them also that love thy name be joyful in thee.

Psalm 5:11

When with his smiles my soul he designs to bless,
Nor cares nor crosses can my peace destroy,
Possessing all things if I him possess,
Enjoying all things if I him enjoy.

Lincoln left an enormous legacy. But he was humble enough to know that anybody can leave a heritage to be celebrated. "I am a living witness that any one of your children may look to come here, to the White House, as my father's child has," he said. Abraham Lincoln was a living testimony that anybody from any background can achieve greatness. Instead of basking in his own light, he encouraged other people to become their own living witness. Your life is a living testimony to others, especially to your friends and family.

Prepare for Your Destiny

Blessed is the people that know the joyful sound: they shall walk, O LORD, in the light of thy countenance.

Psalm 89:15

Bless'd are the souls that hear and know
The gospel's joyful sound;
Peace shall attend the path they go,
And light their steps surround.

Long before he was elected president, Lincoln told a friend why he always worked so hard. "I'll study and get ready, and then the chance will come," he said. Lincoln felt that if he worked hard enough and was well enough prepared, destiny would someday give him a chance. What if he hadn't prepared? He certainly had no idea what God would have for him, but he would be ready when it came. Are you preparing for what God might have for you? Just because your destiny hasn't arrived yet is no cause to be lazy. Try, like Lincoln, to prepare yourself. Get ready for God's appointed time. If you don't, you may miss your opportunity.

Be Impartial

We also joy in God through our Lord Jesus Christ, by whom
we have now received the atonement.

Romans 5:11

> *There is a fountain fill'd with blood,*
> *Drawn from Immanuel's veins,*
> *And sinners plunged beneath that flood*
> *Lose all their guilty stains.*
>
> *The dying thief rejoic'd to see*
> *That fountain in his day;*
> *And here may I, though vile as he,*
> *Wash all my sins away.*

Lincoln believed in being even-handed. "I don't want to be
unjustly accused of dealing illiberally or unfairly with an adversary, either in court, or in a political canvass, or anywhere else,"
he said. "I would despise myself if I supposed myself ready
to deal less liberally with an adversary than I was willing to be
treated myself." Lincoln lived his life by the golden rule, treat-
ing others as he would like to be treated. His unbiased approach
to life gave him the respect he needed to make important decisions. The country trusted him. Are you an impartial judge of
people and situations? If you can develop an unprejudiced
worldview, people will come to you to make their decisions.

Admit When You're Wrong

Be glad in the LORD, and rejoice, ye righteous: and shout for joy, all ye that are upright in heart.

Psalm 32:11

Let those refuse to sing
Who never knew the Lord;
But children of the heavenly King
Should speak their joys abroad.

Lincoln was an honest man, and he wasn't too big to take back his words if he misstated a fact or made an error in his judgment. He did so happily, with a contrite heart. "I have always wanted to deal with everyone I meet candidly and honestly," he said. "If I have made any assertion not warranted by facts, and it is pointed out to me, I will withdraw it cheerfully." Lincoln wasn't ashamed to admit he was wrong, because his confidence did not rely on what others thought of him. Are you stubborn, afraid to admit a mistake? You will gain more confidence by simply admitting when you're wrong. People won't think less of you. In fact, they will think more.

If You Can't Be Honest, Quit

Hitherto have ye asked nothing in my name: ask, and ye shall receive, that your joy may be full.

John 16:24

Dark and cheerless is the morn,
Unaccompanied by thee;
Joyless is the day's return,
Till thy mercy's beams we see:
Day-spring from on high, be near;
Day-star, in our hearts appear.

Honesty was so important to Lincoln that he believed, when in a contest, it was better to give up than to lie. Acting as a mentor to a young attorney, he said, "Resolve to be honest at all events; and if in your judgment you cannot be an honest lawyer, resolve to be honest without being a lawyer. Choose some other occupation, rather than one in the choosing of which you do, in advance, consent to be a knave." Finding the truth and living it was paramount to Lincoln. Have you found yourself telling lies to keep your job, your spouse, or your church? If life gets to a point where you have to lie to keep your position, maybe it's time to quit what you're doing and refocus your life.

Don't Be Deceived

These things have I spoken unto you, that my joy might remain in you, and that your joy might be full.

John 15:11

Art thou not mine, my living Lord?
And can my hope, my comfort die,
Fix'd on thine everlasting word —
The word that built the earth and sky.

As a politician, Lincoln saw a lot of men swindle their way to the top. Early on, he decided to take a different road. "I am glad of all the support I can get anywhere," he said as a young Illinois congressman, "if I can get it without practicing any deception to obtain it." To Lincoln the means was as important as the end, and he refused to use corrupt means to get to the end. Do you have to cheat your way to the top? Integrity means being honest with other people at all times, not just when it serves to better your current position. Lincoln refused to deceive others on his climb to the top, and his integrity served to promote his purposes. It will do the same for you.

Make Plain Your Plans

There be many that say, Who will shew us any good? LORD, lift thou up the light of thy countenance upon us. Thou hast put gladness in my heart, more than in the time that their corn and their wine increased.

Psalm 4:6–7

Lord, what is life? If spent with thee,
In humble praise and prayer,
How long or short my life may be
I feel no anxious care:
Though life depart, my joys shall last,
When life and all its joys are past.

President Lincoln was straightforward in his dealings with others. He sought to be plainly understood. When he took the Oval Office, he presented himself and his plans to Congress simply, without convolution. He had no hidden agendas. "I wish at all times in no way to practice any fraud upon the House or the committee," he said, "and I also desire to do nothing which may be very disagreeable to any of the members of Congress." Are you frank with other people, or do you leave room for doubt? People who are fuzzy in their words and actions leave too much room for uncertainty. Be straightforward with people.

Advocate the Truth

Love ye your enemies, and do good, and lend, hoping for nothing again; and your reward shall be great, and ye shall be the children of the Highest: for he is kind unto the unthankful and to the evil.

Luke 6:35

> *Lord, shall thy bright example shine*
> *In vain before my eyes?*
> *Give me a soul akin to thine,*
> *To love my enemies.*

Lincoln believed so strongly in the truth, he was willing to give the supreme sacrifice—his life. He drew the battle line on the principles of justice and freedom. "If it is decreed that I should go down because of this speech, then let me go down linked to the truth. Let me die in the advocacy of what is just and right," he said. Lincoln's willingness to sacrifice his life gave the country confidence. It was his willingness to die that helped the Union make sacrifices to fight for freedom and justice. Are you willing to die for the truth? Where have you drawn your own battle lines? Take a position in life and let the world know that is where you stand. Be willing to make the ultimate sacrifice, and everyone around you will join your cause.

Stand for the Truth

Forbearing one another, and forgiving one another, if any man
have a quarrel against any: even as Christ forgave you, so also
do ye.

Colossians 3:13

May we each with each agree,
Through thy uniting grace:
Our gift shall thine accepted be,
Our life be love and praise.

Perhaps one of Lincoln's greatest strengths was his inflexible defense of the truth. To Lincoln, the truth wasn't flexible,
and he made it clear to all that he wouldn't stand for anything
but the truth. He couldn't be coaxed or bribed, and he asked
everyone else to do the same. "Stand with anybody that stands
right. Stand with him while he is right, and part with him
when he goes wrong," observed Lincoln. Sometimes in life you
have to part ways with those who take the low road. Do you put
up with dishonest people in your life? At times you have to
part with those who compromise their integrity, or you'll lose
your own.

Stick to Your Word

Judge not, that ye be not judged. . . . Why beholdest thou the
mote that is in thy brother's eye, but considerest not the beam
that is in thine own eye?

Matthew 7:1, 3

Make us by thy transforming grace,
Great Saviour, daily more like thee:
Thy fair example may we trace,
To teach us what we ought to be.

It is one thing to make a promise but quite another to make
a promise on behalf of another person. When Lincoln
promised that the Union would fight for the cause of freedom, he knew it was a promise made by all and thus important to keep. "I make a point of honor and conscience in all
things to stick to my word, especially if others had been
induced to act on it," said Lincoln. Do you guard the vows
you have made in behalf of other people? Many times we make
promises that affect others in our lives—our spouses, children, or employers. Guard these vows, because if they are broken, you're not the only one who will get hurt.

Happiness Is Action

If thine enemy hunger, feed him: if he thirst, give him drink: for in so doing thou shalt heap coals of fire on his head. Be not overcome of evil, but overcome evil with good.

Romans 12:20–21

> *Thus artists melt the sullen ore of lead,*
> *With heaping coals of fire upon its head;*
> *In the kind warmth the metal learns to glow,*
> *And loose from dross the silver runs below.*

Because of his frontier upbringing, Abraham Lincoln was no stranger to work. Growing up in the woods required hard labor simply to survive. His work ethic never left him as an adult, and his resourcefulness caused others around him to work hard too. "Work, work, work, is the main thing," he said. It's what made him happy. If you're depressed, have you tried simply working harder? To Lincoln, work was not only important for survival; it was the very thing that brought happiness. It's hard to stay focused on what's wrong with your life when you're busy taking action.

Lean on God

Being justified by faith, we have peace with God through our Lord Jesus Christ.

Romans 5:1

No fiery vengeance now,
Nor burning wrath comes down;
If justice call for sinners' blood,
The Saviour shows his own.

During the darkest days of the Civil War, Abraham Lincoln was confronted by trouble on all sides. "Encompassed by vast difficulties as I am, nothing shall be wanting on my part," he insisted, "if sustained by God and the American people." The president made it clear that it was only by God's help that he made it through tough times. God supplied all his needs. Are you surrounded on all sides by trouble? Whom are you leaning on for help? There's only one place to find your sustenance, and it's the same place Lincoln went for help—God. When you make your Maker the one to whom you go for help, you'll have no room left for anxiety. No difficulty is too vast for God.

Give a Graceful Way Out

Thou wilt keep him in perfect peace, whose mind is stayed on thee: because he trusteth in thee.

Isaiah 26:3

Saviour, on earth I covet not
That every woe should cease;
Only, if trouble be my lot,
In thee let me have peace.

Over the course of his life, Lincoln not only learned to for-give and forget, but he did so in biblical proportions. He was world renowned for his compassion. "I am a patient man—always willing to forgive on the Christian terms of repentance; and also to give ample time for repentance," he wrote. It was God's Word that helped Lincoln learn to be so benevolent. And it was the Bible that caused Lincoln to be slow to judge and quick to repent and forgive. Do you give other people grace? Do you expect others to ask for forgiveness right away, or are you willing to give time even for the most obstinate? Lincoln gave a graceful way out, the same way God gives.

Do Nothing in Malice

Be perfect, be of good comfort, be of one mind, live in peace; and the God of love and peace shall be with you.

2 Corinthians 13:11

Make us of one heart and mind,
Courteous, pitiful, and kind;
Lowly, meek in thought and word,
Altogether like our Lord.

Abraham Lincoln was a gentle man. At the same time, he was a diligent and persistent military commander. These characteristics might seem to be at odds. But Lincoln's mild manner actually gave him the respect he needed to talk tough and carry a big stick. He was determined but not cruel. "I shall do nothing in malice," he proclaimed. "What I deal with is too vast for malicious dealing." Because the country believed Lincoln acted out of principle and not out of self-promotion or political expediency, he gained the support he needed to wage war. Do you act out of spite or principle? If you act out of malice, you'll soon lose the support you need. If you act out of love and for the truth, you'll never have to look around for support.

Be Lenient

Peace be within thy walls, and prosperity within thy palaces.

Psalm 122:7

For our dear brethren's sake,
Zion, we wish thee peace;
Prosper, oh! prosper long,
And may thy sons increase:
We seek thy good, we love the road
Which leads us to God's bless'd abode.

President Lincoln granted so many pardons during the war that he was jokingly referred to as "His Leniency." Lincoln's sympathetic manner stirred some alarm among his military commanders. "Some of my generals complain that I impair discipline by my frequent pardons," he said. "But it rests me, after a day's hard work, if I can find some excuse for saving some poor fellow's life, and I shall go to bed happy tonight as I think how joyous the signing of this name will make himself, his family, and friends." Do you leave room for leniency? We all make mistakes in life, and we all are grateful for those who are lenient with us. In fact, we can probably all remember times when someone else's leniency helped us grow.

Let God Be Your Judge

If it be possible, as much as lieth in you, live peaceably with all men.

Romans 12:18

*His purpose is that we should bear
His image now on earth,
And by our peaceful lives declare
Our new and heavenly birth.*

Being belittled by someone is difficult to bear. Most people can't stand to be vilified. They cave in. Lincoln learned to stand his ground, to hold fast to his convictions, but only with the help of his Maker. "I can only say that I have acted upon my best convictions, without selfishness or malice, and that by the help of God I shall continue to do so," he admitted. Only by God's grace was Lincoln able to withstand criticism. Who's your judge, God or other people? If you look too much to other people, you'll never find the support you need. But you can have the confidence that God won't put you down. If you stand for the truth, God will promote you, not demote you, just as he did Lincoln.

Be Devoted to Your Cause

He that overcometh shall inherit all things; and I will be his God, and he shall be my son.

Revelation 21:7

The saints in his presence receive
Their great and eternal reward;
With Jesus in heaven they live;
They reign in the smile of their Lord.

When confronted with the possibility of failure, Lincoln dug in. He became more diligent, even when others recommended he quit. "I expect to maintain this contest until successful, or till I die, or am conquered, or my term expires, or Congress or the country forsakes me," he proclaimed. Lincoln's devotion stirred the spirits of his fellow Americans. It gave the country the courage to withstand its suffering. Are you devoted to your cause? Lincoln named all the ways he might ultimately lose, even to death. But, it was his resoluteness that helped the rest of the country to dig in too. If you devote yourself entirely to your cause, you'll be surprised at how many other people will join you.

Don't Be Diverted

No man can serve two masters: for either he will hate the one, and love the other; or else he will hold to the one, and despise the other. Ye cannot serve God and mammon.

Matthew 6:24

Not a broken, brief obedience
Does the Lord of heaven demand;
He requires our whole allegiance,
Words and deeds, and heart and hand:
God will hold divided sway
With no deity of clay.

A young military cadet once asked Lincoln how to best get ahead in life. Lincoln's advice was not only to ignore his critics, but to simply imagine there were none. "The way for a young man to rise is to improve himself every way he can, never suspecting that anybody wishes to hinder him," he wrote. He told the young man to forge a path uninhibited by the objections of others. Are you dissuaded by the possibility of criticism, afraid to act because of what others might say? Lincoln believed the way to success was to be so optimistic as to think nobody would stand in your way. Lincoln took a stand and ignored his critics. Follow his example. Don't be diverted!

Take Your Time

Oh how great is thy goodness, which thou hast laid up for
them that fear thee; which thou hast wrought for them that
trust in thee before the sons of men!

Psalm 31:19

This is the hope that shall sustain me
Till life's pilgrimage be past;
Fears may vex, and troubles pain me,
I shall reach my home at last.

Lincoln wasn't hasty. "Nothing valuable can be lost by taking time," he warned. If a thing was to be done right, it took
staying power. If a goal was important, if it was the right thing
to do, then prudence dictated that it be done in due time. Life
presents itself with all sorts of opportunities, good and bad
choices. Lincoln believed, "If there be an object to hurry any
of you, in haste, to a step which you would never take delib-
erately, that object will be frustrated by taking time; but no
good object can be frustrated by it." Are you impatient to reach
your goals? If there is something you aim to do, take your time
and do it right. According to Lincoln, the thing you want will
be there if it's worthwhile.

Keep Every Promise

I will behold thy face in righteousness: I shall be satisfied, when I awake, with thy likeness.

Psalm 17:15

Oh! when awaken'd by thy care,
Thy face I view, thy image bear,
How shall my breast with transport glow!
What full delight my heart o'erflow!

If Lincoln was known for anything, it was that he kept his word. Today, generations later, he's still known for the vows he kept. How important was honesty to Abe Lincoln? "If you make a bad bargain, hug it all the tighter," he wrote. Some people keep the promises that benefit them and break those that don't. For Lincoln, honesty was nonnegotiable. Even if he made a promise that, in the end, wasn't any good, he still kept his word. Do you keep only the promises that help you? If so, then none of your promises is taken very seriously. Integrity is a full-time job and doesn't leave room for vacations. Being honest all the time is hard work, but the end result—being trusted all the time—will give you a legacy like Lincoln's.

What to Do When Ridiculed

Master, what shall I do to inherit eternal life? . . . And he
answering said, Thou shalt love the Lord thy God with all thy
heart, and with all thy soul, and with all thy strength, and
with all thy mind.

Luke 10:25, 27

Yes, I would love thee, blessed God!
Paternal goodness marks thy name;
Thy praises, through thy high abode,
The heavenly hosts with joy proclaim.

If you don't expect to find any criticism in life, you'll be sorely
disappointed. Lincoln knew it was coming and got used to it.
"I have endured a great deal of ridicule without much malice
and have received a great deal of kindness, not quite free from
ridicule. I am used to it," he said. If you make up your mind
to expect to be criticized, then maybe the ridicule won't hurt
so much. Are you surprised by criticism? Are you taken off-
guard when somebody says something disparaging? Lincoln
got used to the criticism, so it didn't impede his progress. The
best thing to do right now is to get used to being criticized. If
you do, it won't hurt you as much.

On Blame

Mark the perfect man, and behold the upright: for the end of that man is peace.

Psalm 37:37

> *How bless'd the righteous when he dies,*
> *When sinks a weary soul to rest!*
> *How mildly beam the closing eyes!*
> *How gently heaves the' expiring breast!*
>
> *Life's labour done, as sinks the clay,*
> *Light from its load the spirit flies;*
> *While heaven and earth combine to say,*
> *"How bless'd the righteous when he dies!"*

When things aren't going the way we expected, it's easy to blame others. When Lincoln was opposed for a second term in the Oval Office, he politely reminded the country that it wasn't his doing that got the country in trouble. He didn't claim to be the ideal leader, but he did remind them not to jump ship out of fear that the ship might sink. "I have not permitted myself, gentlemen, to conclude that I am the best man in the country; but I am reminded, in this connection, of a story of a farmer, who remarked to a companion once that it is not best to swap horses when crossing streams." Do you blame others for your problems and then ditch those people just when you need them most?

Be Transparent

Knowing the time, that now it is high time to awake out of sleep: for now is our salvation nearer than when we believed.

Romans 13:11

The time is short, but who can tell
How short his time below may be?
To-day on earth his soul may dwell,
To-morrow in eternity.

Part of being sincere is to be totally pure in actions and deeds and thus to be clearly understood. "I [wish to be] so clear," Lincoln wrote, "no honest man can misunderstand me and no dishonest one successfully misrepresent me." Lincoln's simplicity caused other people around him to trust him and to be transparent in their dealings with him. He left no room for confusion or doubt. It was his simple approach to life and business that made other people trust him. Are you transparent in all you do? Or do you leave room for suspicion? It's hard to be trusted if you don't give straight answers. Try to be unambiguous in life, making your plans plain to everyone who comes in contact with you.

Work on Your Character

Our light affliction, which is but for a moment, worketh for us a far more exceeding and eternal weight of glory.

2 Corinthians 4:17

All trials and sorrows the Christian prepare
For the rest that remaineth above;
On earth tribulation awaits him, but there
The smile of unchangeable love.

Lincoln spent a great deal of time developing his character. For him, strong moral fiber wasn't something that just happened. It was something you worked on. Like a tree in a forest, character grows with the proper nourishment. "A man's character is like a tree and his reputation like its shadow; the shadow is what we think of it; the tree is the real thing," he said. Do you work on your character, striving to improve it and to build your integrity? Lincoln made a point to work on his character by praying, by reading the Bible and other virtuous books, and by learning all he could. Character development was something he viewed as purposeful, not incidental. Don't let your character grow only by accident.

Earn Their Respect

Forasmuch as ye know that ye were not redeemed with corruptible things, as silver and gold . . . but with the precious blood of Christ, as of a lamb without blemish and without spot.

1 Peter 1:18–19

Our sins and griefs on him were laid;
He meekly bore the mighty load:
Our ransom price he fully paid,
By offering up himself to God.

Contrary to popular opinion, respect is not necessarily earned by intelligence, charm, or power. According to Abraham Lincoln, all it takes is sincerity. "The world shall know that I will keep my faith to friends and enemies, come what will," wrote Lincoln. And the world did know and came to respect him for it. What we remember Lincoln for today isn't a magnetic personality or genius-like intelligence; rather, we remember him for his honest and humble approach to life and work. He was authentic. Are you trying the hard way to get respect, or have you tried the easy way—to tell the truth? Having integrity and dealing honestly are the easiest ways to earn respect.

Learn—Don't Avenge

I am crucified with Christ: nevertheless I live; yet not I, but Christ liveth in me: and the life which I now live in the flesh I live by the faith of the Son of God.

Galatians 2:20

> *Close to the ignominious tree,*
> *Jesus, my humbled soul would cleave;*
> *Despised and crucified with thee,*
> *With Christ resolved to die and live:*
> *There would I bow my suppliant knee,*
> *And own no other Lord but thee.*

Lincoln put out the fires of revenge. He called for the Union not to settle the score but instead to learn from its mistakes. "Human nature will not change," he wrote near the end of the war. "In any future great national trial, compared with the men of this, we shall have as weak and as strong, as silly and as wise, as bad and as good. Let us therefore study the incidents of this, as philosophy to learn wisdom from, and none of them as wrongs to be revenged." Do you heal scars or let them bleed? Lincoln aspired to make the Civil War a learning experience, to take all that had happened and reconstruct a better life for all. After your battles have been waged, learn from the experiences instead of taking revenge.

Change the World

I beseech you therefore, brethren, by the mercies of God, that ye present your bodies a living sacrifice, holy, acceptable unto God, which is your reasonable service.

Romans 12:1

Thine, wholly thine, I want to be;
The sacrifice receive:
Made, and preserved, and saved by thee,
To thee myself I give.

"I have an irrepressible desire to live till I can be assured that the world is a little better for my having lived in it," Lincoln wrote as president. Many people give up on the possibility of changing the world. Lincoln, however, never gave up. His aim was to make the world a better place, a place with freedom and justice for all. It was that selfless goal that eventually led to his own demise. But he accomplished his desires, and even today he's known for his indelible mark on America and the world. Have you given up on changing the world? Go ahead, be idealistic enough to believe you can make a difference.

Friendships Endure

If any man will come after me, let him deny himself, and take up his cross daily, and follow me.

Luke 9:23

> *Take up thy cross, let not its weight*
> *Fill thy weak spirit with alarm,*
> *My strength shall bear thy spirit up,*
> *And brace thy heart, and nerve thy arm.*

> *Take up thy cross, and follow me,*
> *Nor think till death to lay it down;*
> *For only he who bears the cross*
> *May hope to wear the glorious crown.*

Lincoln never forgot his friends. They were important to him. In spite of the war, he even refused to let go of his friends in the South. "We are not enemies but friends," he insisted in a letter to a rebel friend. "We must not be enemies. Though passion may have strained, it must not break our bonds of affection." The significance of friendship endured even through bloodshed. It was the very thing that helped keep the country together even while at war. Have you given up on old friends because of disagreements or separation? Lincoln believed a friendship could survive heated battles, dogged disagreements, and even the killing fields. He pursued them relentlessly. Will you?

Don't Bask in Your Glory

Yea doubtless, and I count all things but loss for the excellency of the knowledge of Christ Jesus my Lord: for whom I have suffered the loss of all things, and do count them but dung, that I may win Christ.

Philippians 3:8

On thee alone my hope relies;
Beneath the cross I fall,
My Lord, my life, my sacrifice,
My Saviour, and my all.

Even when the Union won the war, Lincoln didn't bask long in the glory of his victory. He tempered talks of defeating the enemy with conciliatory language. "In all our rejoicings, let us neither express nor cherish any hard feelings toward any citizen who, by his vote, has differed with us. Let us at all times remember that all American citizens are brothers of common country, and should do well together in the bonds of fraternal feeling," he wrote. If Lincoln were to brag about anything, it would be that he *found* his long-lost friends in the South, not that he beat them. Do you "rub noses in the dirt," or do you make up with other people after a disagreement? Bask in the glory too long, and you may not have any friends left.

Rely on God's Gifts

All things are lawful for me, but all things are not expedient: all things are lawful for me, but all things edify not.

1 Corinthians 10:23

Lord, ever let me freely yield
What most I prize to thee,
Who never hast a good withheld,
Or wilt withhold from me.

Thy favour all my journey through,
Thou art engaged to grant;
What else I want or think I do,
'Tis better still to want.

When the going gets tough, how do you renew your strength? When the Union was running out of enthusiasm for the war effort, Lincoln harkened them back to the original source of their strength. "Our reliance," he said, "is in the love of liberty which God has planted in our bosoms." President Lincoln reminded Americans of their original purpose, that the defense of freedom and justice was what made America strong. How do *you* find the energy to endure, and the strength to survive? Don't forget to rely on the things God has planted inside of you. Go there to renew your spirit.

God's Justice Prevails

Whereto we have already attained, let us walk by the same rule, let us mind the same thing.

Philippians 3:16

Bound to one Lord, by common vow
In one great enterprize;
One faith, one hope, one centre now,
Our common home, the skies.

According to Lincoln, God has fundamental principles that just can't be avoided. These are the things we should reply on and fight for. According to Lincoln, justice was rooted in God's sovereignty. It was something God ordained. "Those who deny freedom to others deserve it not for themselves; and, under a just God, cannot long retain it," he said. There was no running away from justice, Lincoln implied, because God intended all men to live in freedom and liberty. You can't run away from God and his purposes, not for long. Are you running from God and his will? Remember, his purposes always prevail.

Value Life

I beseech you, brethren, by the name of our Lord Jesus Christ, that ye all speak the same thing, and that there be no divisions among you; but that ye be perfectly joined together in the same mind and in the same judgment.

1 Corinthians 1:10

> *Lord, subdue our selfish will,*
> *Each to each our temper suit,*
> *By thy modulating skill,*
>   *Heart to heart, as lute to lute.*

As commander in chief, Lincoln sent thousands of young men to their death on the battlefield. But he never gave up the chance to be compassionate, even to save a life if possible. "If a man had more than one life, I think a little hanging would not hurt this one, but after he is once dead, we cannot bring him back, no matter how sorry we may be, so the boy shall be pardoned," he wrote when saving the life of a young rebel soldier. Perhaps because Lincoln experienced so much grief in his own life, he gained an appreciation for life's temporal nature. Do you value life? Life on earth can be short, so whatever can be done should be done to guard it.

Never Surrender

Where two or three are gathered together in my name, there am I in the midst of them.

Matthew 18:20

> *Where two or three with sweet accord,*
> *Obedient to their sovereign Lord,*
> *Meet to recount his acts of grace,*
> *And offer solemn prayer and praise;*
> *There, saith the Saviour, will I be*
> *Amid the little company.*

Lincoln was unremitting in the task of winning the Civil War. His doggedness became legendary. "The fight must go on," he declared. "The cause of civil liberty must not be surrendered at the end of one or even one hundred defeats." It was Lincoln's persistence that gave the Union the confidence and persistence to push Robert E. Lee and his generals back. Surrender was no option for Lincoln, to the point that he was willing to give up his own life. Have you raised the white flag in your life? If you decide now to never surrender, chances are you'll ultimately gain the victory.

Look at a Person's Heart

Teaching and admonishing one another in psalms and hymns and spiritual songs, singing with grace in your hearts to the Lord.

Colossians 3:16

Teach us, though in a world of sin,
Heaven's bless'd employment to begin,
To sing our great Redeemer's praise;
And love his name, and learn his ways.

Outward appearances can be deceiving. It's what's inside—one's motives and character—that matters most. Lincoln observed this throughout life, perhaps because he was so unattractive and unbecoming! He was nothing special to look at, but according to Lincoln, "Common-looking people are the best in the world; that is the reason the Lord makes so many of them." Despite Lincoln's awkward appearance, his confidence stood supreme. He looked inward, not outward. Do you value inward or outward appearances more? If you value outward appearances more highly, you may have passed right over Abraham Lincoln if you had had the chance to hire him or choose him for a friend. Look inside a person to discover what he or she really is made of.

Love Your Enemies

Abstain from all appearance of evil.

1 Thessalonians 5:22

Our Saviour by a heavenly birth
Calls us to holiness on earth,
Bids us our former follies hate,
And from the wicked separate.

We must have holy hearts and hands,
And feet that go where he commands;
A holy will to keep his ways,
And holy lips to speak his praise.

Lincoln didn't enjoy tromping all over people. He had no desire to climb the ladder at someone else's expense. "It is no pleasure to me to triumph over anyone," he said. Lincoln admonished others to stand for what was true without putting other people down. His humble, poverty-stricken conditions probably served him well, giving him the view from the bottom of the barrel. He saw life from an underdog's perspective, and he had no appreciation for those who tried to keep a man down. Do you gloat in the defeat of another? Try loving your enemies, because someday you may be the defeated one looking for a friend.

Hold Your Temper

Let every one that nameth the name of Christ depart from iniquity.

2 Timothy 2:19

Faith must obey her Father's will,
As well as trust his grace;
A pardoning God is jealous still
For his own holiness.

"Quarrel not at all," Lincoln said. President Lincoln restrained himself from losing his temper, and he advised his colleagues to do the same. "No man resolved to make the most of himself can spare time for personal contention. Still less can he afford to take all the consequences, including the wanting of his temper and the loss of self-control." Self-control and moderation were important to Lincoln. He valued his time and refused to waste it on things that didn't help him attain his goals. How much energy do you waste by losing your temper? It's hard to keep focused on your goals if you lose control or use up your energy in a fight. In all things, be moderate.

Choose Your Battles Wisely

Lest Satan should get an advantage of us: for we are not ignorant of his devices.

2 Corinthians 2:11

Fear not Satan's strong temptations
Though they tease thee day by day,
And thy evil inclinations
Overwhelm thee with dismay!
Thou shalt conquer,
Through the Lamb's redeeming blood.

Rightly choosing what to fight for and what to let go was one of Lincoln's strengths. "Yield larger things to which you can show no more than equal right; and yield lesser ones, though clearly your own," he wrote. While some people contend for everything and try to show up others at just about everything they do, Lincoln was satisfied with winning only those battles that mattered. "It's better to give your path to a dog than be bitten by him in contesting for the right. Even killing the dog would not cure the bite." Are you always fighting for your rights? Sometimes it's best to give up and let someone else win a battle. If you're going to win your war, you have to choose your battles wisely.

Be a Peacemaker

I find then a law, that, when I would do good, evil is present with me.

Romans 7:21

> *Oh! who can free my troubled mind*
> *From sin's oppressive load?*
> *O wretched man! how shall I find*
> *Acceptance with my God?*
>
> *My soul with transport turns to thee,*
> *To thee my Saviour turns;*
> *Cleansed by thy blood, and saved by grace,*
> *My soul no longer mourns.*

When Lincoln was caught between two sides in an argument, he refused to jump in right away. Instead, he helped the disputants understand each other and get over their disagreement. "When I have friends who disagree with each other, I am very slow to take sides in their quarrel," he told a constituent. Lincoln looked for harmony. Ironically, the man who led the country through the gravest war in American history was, by nature, a peacemaker. Maybe that's why he was able to hold the nation together. Are you a peacemaker or a war wager? Those who help keep the peace are often the ones called to lead. The spirit of compromise wins wars.

Think It Through

Lead us not into temptation, but deliver us from evil.

Matthew 6:13

Protect us in the dangerous hour,
And from the wily tempter's power,
Lord, set our spirits free;
And if temptation should assail
May mighty grace o'er all prevail,
And lead our hearts to thee.

Don't act too fast. That was Lincoln's philosophy. He was introspective, and he liked to ponder things before making a move. He would investigate, research, pray, and ask others for their opinion. "I am never easy now, when I am handling a thought, till I have bounded it north and bounded it south, and bounded it east and bounded it west," he explained. It's easy to act fast, to move on intuition, but later we may regret it. Taking a little more time to make a decision can make all the difference, especially when in prayer. Do you act too fast, or do you take time to think? Before making your next decision, make sure you take the time to look at it from all sides.

Finish What You Start

Enter not into the path of the wicked, and go not in the way of evil men. Avoid it, pass not by it, turn from it, and pass away.

Proverbs 4:14–15

A wicked world and wicked heart
With Satan are combined:
Each acts a too successful part,
In harassing my mind.

But fighting in my Saviour's strength,
Though mighty are my foes,
I shall a conqueror be at length
O'er all that can oppose.

Abraham Lincoln had a pet peeve: quitting halfway through a project. Perhaps his strong work ethic, developed as a child, caused him to work so hard to complete a task. "Half-finished work generally proves to be labor lost," he said. We should appreciate Lincoln's rigid, finish-a-job-started attitude, because it was his persistence that helped the Union finish its job. We can also cultivate this character trait in our own personal lives. How many jobs have you started but not finished? For every job you fail to complete, you have lost all the time it took to get started. If you make up your mind ahead of time, there's no telling how much you can accomplish if you just finish what you started.

Value Your Friendships

Be ye kind one to another, tenderhearted, forgiving one another, even as God for Christ's sake hath forgiven you.

Ephesians 4:32

"Is Christ divided?" What can part
The members from the Head?
Oh, how should those be one in heart
For whom our Saviour bled?

Abraham Lincoln enjoyed companionship more than most people do. Spending time with others in conversation or leisure was important to him. He valued friendship above almost everything else in his life. And for all of his hard work, he always found time to spend with his friends. "The better part of one's life consists of his friendships," he said. This rare display of friendship spoke volumes about Lincoln and his character. To be a good friend takes sincerity and integrity and the ability to enjoy oneself. Do you value friendships? If not, why not?

Don't Procrastinate

I myself am persuaded of you, my brethren, that ye also are full of goodness, filled with all knowledge, able also to admonish one another.

Romans 15:14

Bonds of everlasting love
Draw our souls in union,
To our Father's house above,
To the saints' communion.
Thither may our hopes ascend,
There may all our labours end.

Throughout his life, Lincoln was always one to press on. He didn't delay, and he didn't put things off. It was a lesson he learned as a child from the Bible. "See'st thou a man diligent in his business and he shall stand before kings," he would quote to his law partner from the Book of Proverbs. Those who dawdled their way through life wouldn't amount to much, according to Lincoln. "The leading rule for the lawyer," he said, "as for the man of every other calling, is diligence." Leave nothing for tomorrow that can be done today. Do you procrastinate? Be diligent to work through things rather than putting them off.

What It Means to Be Godly

Comfort yourselves together, and edify one another, even as also ye do.

1 Thessalonians 5:11

While we journey, let us
Help each other on the road;
Foes on every side beset us,
Snares through all the way are strew'd:
It behooves us,
Each to bear a brother's load.

What's the definition of godliness? For Lincoln, it wasn't piousness or churchgoing. The righteous, the eternally rewarded, was the person who knew the truth and lived a life of sincerity. "In very truth, he was the noblest work of God—an honest man," he wrote to the widow of a soldier killed in action. Lincoln esteemed honesty above all else. To "have religion" meant little to Abraham Lincoln if a person wasn't true to himself. That was a principle he learned from the Bible, and it stuck with him throughout his life. Is your word your honor? Guard it, and you can be sure you'll too be recognized as a noble work of God.

Let God Decide

Pray one for another. . . . The effectual fervent prayer of a righteous man availeth much.

James 5:16

Before our Father's throne
We pour our ardent prayers;
Our fears, our hopes, our aims are one —
Our comforts and our cares.

Every day we make choices—some good and some bad. Sometimes even the most trivial decisions change the direction of our lives. What did Abraham Lincoln do when he had to make a choice? "Amid the greatest difficulties of my administration," he explained, "when I could not see any other resort, I would place my whole reliance in God, knowing that all would go well, and that he would decide for the right." Lincoln went to God, and because he went to God, he didn't worry about making the wrong choices. Do you let God decide, or do you try to take matters into your own hands? When you rely on God to give you the wisdom to make good decisions, like Lincoln, you'll decide for the right.

Be on God's Side

Be content with such things as ye have: for he hath said, I will never leave thee, nor forsake thee.

Hebrews 13:5

Since he has said, "I'll ne'er depart,"
I'll bind his promise to my heart,
Rejoicing in his care:
This shall support while here I live,
And, when in glory I arrive,
Will praise him for it there.

Lincoln was sure God was on his side. His confidence in the righteousness of his case was unshakable. What he worried about was whether he was on God's side. He worried that his integrity, diligence in prayer, and character weren't worthy of God's holiness. "I am not at all concerned that the Lord is on the North's side in the war, for I know the Lord is always on the side of the *right*. But it is my constant anxiety and prayer that I and this nation should be on the Lord's side," he said. Lincoln recognized the awesome responsibility of being used by God, and he feared not living up to the responsibility. Are you on God's side? If you believe God is on your side, make sure you're on his.

With God, Who Can Be Against You?

There is no soundness in my flesh because of thine anger; neither is there any rest in my bones because of my sin. For mine iniquities are gone over mine head: as an heavy burden they are too heavy for me.

Psalm 38:3–4

> *O Thou that hear'st the prayer of faith,*
> *Wilt thou not save my soul from death,*
> *My soul that rests on thee?*
> *I have no refuge of my own,*
> *But fly to what my Lord hath done*
> *And suffer'd once for me.*

Abraham Lincoln had great faith. "If we do right God will be with us, and if God is with us we cannot fail," he declared. Lincoln's unshakable faith was a testimony not only to his own troops and to the Union, but to the enemy as well. There was no doubt that Lincoln was in for the long haul. He believed that God would not let him down. He stood firm, and nobody or nothing could stand against God. Ultimately, Lincoln was right. What is the measure of your faith in God? Do you believe in earnest that God will stand by you to the end, until you see your promised land?

Acknowledge God's Wisdom

Godly sorrow worketh repentance to salvation not to be repented of: but the sorrow of the world worketh death.

2 Corinthians 7:10

My lips with shame my sins confess
Against thy law, against thy grace:
Lo, should thy judgments grow severe,
I am condemn'd, but thou art clear.

When Lincoln had self-doubts, he would remind himself that God's wisdom prevails. When the war was going badly for the Union, he wrote, "We hoped for a happy termination of this terrible war long before this; but God knows best and has ruled otherwise. We shall yet acknowledge his wisdom and our own error therein. Meanwhile we must work earnestly in the best light he gives us, trusting that so working still conduces to the great ends he ordains." When in doubt, do you trust God's wisdom? Even when things don't go your way, if you believe God, you can rest assured God has his reasons.

God Sustains

Whosoever is born of God doth not commit sin; for his seed remaineth in him: and he cannot sin, because he is born of God.

1 John 3:9

Oh! give me, Lord, the tender heart
That trembles at the' approach of sin,
A godly fear of sin impart,
Implant and root it deep within.

When Lincoln faced the duties of the Oval Office, he knew it was a job too big for any single person. He exclaimed, "I should be the most presumptuous blockhead upon this footstool if I for one day thought that I should discharge the duties which have come upon me without the aid and enlightenment of One who is stronger and wiser than all others." Lincoln relied on God, not on his cabinet or generals, to give him the wisdom and strength to govern the country. Do you act like God is stronger and wiser than you? If you're trying to "go it alone" or are living your life based on the views and opinions of others, take Lincoln's lead and rest on the One who is stronger and wiser.

Pray for God's Favor

They that are Christ's have crucified the flesh with the affections and lusts.

Galatians 5:24

Great God, assist me through the fight;
Make me triumphant in thy might:
Thou the desponding heart canst raise;
The victory mine, and thine the praise.

Lincoln sensed the prayers of his fellow Americans. They strengthened him. Frequently when he spoke to citizens in cities across the North, he thanked people for their prayers. "It is most cheering and encouraging," he once observed, "for me to know that in the efforts which I have made and am making for the restoration of a righteous peace to our country, I am upheld and sustained by the good wishes and prayers of God's people." Do you pray for others? Lincoln was buoyed by everyone who prayed for him, because he knew God listened to those prayers. Imagine the feeling of thousands of people praying for you. Imagine God listening to all of those prayers.

In Victory, Don't Forget God

Blessed is he whose transgression is forgiven, whose sin is covered. Blessed is the man unto whom the LORD imputeth not iniquity, and in whose spirit there is no guile.

Psalm 32:1–2

The Saviour smiles! o'er my bless'd soul
New tides of hope tumultuous roll;
Earth has a joy unknown in heaven,
The new-born peace of sin forgiven;
Tears of such pure and deep delight,
Ye angels! never dimm'd your sight.

Although the end of the war could not yet be seen, the Union was piling up victories. Confidence was gaining. But even then Lincoln refused to let the country forget that God was still the one who would give the ultimate victory. "No one is more deeply aware that without his favor our highest wisdom is but as foolishness and that our most strenuous efforts would avail nothing in the shadow of his displeasure," he said. Small victories can be self-defeating when they make you think you've already won the war. Only God gives the ultimate victory. Do you count your victories too soon? Don't be deceived by false confidences. Stay with God until he gives you victory.

Read the Bible

Nevertheless I have somewhat against thee, because thou hast left thy first love. Remember therefore from whence thou art fallen, and repent, and do the first works.

Revelation 2:4–5

I need the influence of thy grace
To speed me in the way,
Lest I should loiter in my pace,
Or turn my feet astray.

We all have favorite books—books that teach and encourage us to reach our goals. The Bible was important to Abraham Lincoln. It was the first book he read and studied as a child, and he reportedly memorized large sections of it. "In regards to this great Book," he wrote to a friend, "I have but to say, it is the best gift God has given to men. All the good Savior gave to this world was communicated through this Book. But for it we could not know right from wrong. All things most desirable for man's welfare, here and hereafter, are to be found portrayed in it." Certainly many of Lincoln's qualities as a leader, including his honesty and humility, were learned from the Bible. It was, in fact, his most important resource. Is the Bible your book of choice?

Let God Lift Your Burden

The LORD said unto Satan, Behold, all that he hath is in thy power; only upon himself put not forth thine hand.

Job 1:12

Still thine integrity hold fast,
The tempter's counsel spurn,
Hope against hope, and God at last,
Will for thy help return.

Sending men to their deaths on the battlefield was hard for Lincoln and his generals. He was reportedly in turmoil at the thought of all the widows and orphans that would result from the war. How did the president bear the thought of it? "Without the assistance of that Divine Being, I cannot succeed. With that assistance, I cannot fail," he once confided to friends in his hometown in Illinois. Do you have someone who can lift your burdens? You can go to the same place President Lincoln went for help when he was weighted down—to God.

Sustained by God's People

Let no man say when he is tempted, I am tempted of God: for God cannot be tempted with evil, neither tempteth he any man: But every man is tempted, when he is drawn away of his own lust, and enticed.

James 1:13–14

My crimes, though great, do not surpass
The power and glory of thy grace;
Oh! wash my soul from every sin,
And make my guilty conscience clean.

President Lincoln looked not only to God but also to God's people for help. Lincoln believed America was a chosen people, a people picked by God to protect the cause of freedom and justice on earth. So when he needed encouragement, he would go to those people whom God had appointed. "It is true . . . that very great responsibility rests upon me in the position to which the votes of the American people have called me. . . . I turn, then, and look to the American people, and to that God who has never forsaken them." Do you turn to God's people for help, asking them to support you? If God gave you a mission, he didn't intend for you to achieve it alone.

The Body of Christ Unites

They that will be rich fall into temptation and a snare, and into many foolish and hurtful lusts, which drown men in destruction and perdition.

1 Timothy 6:9

Oh lay not up upon this earth
Your hopes, your joys, your treasure,
Here sorrow clouds the pilgrim's path,
And blights each opening pleasure.
All, all below must fade and die,
The dearest hopes we cherish,
Scenes touch'd with brightest radiancy,
All are decreed to perish.

Belief in the idea of God, a higher power, was not enough for Abraham Lincoln. He professed faith in the God of the Bible and the New Testament, and it was this faith that helped see him through. "We are bound together in Christianity," he once wrote, ". . . and while some of us may differ in political opinions, we are united in one feeling for the Union. We all believe in the maintenance of the Union, of every star and stripe of the glorious flag." Christ united Lincoln's America. Are you united with others by Christ? The message of salvation, given by Jesus, is the only true source of unity for you, your family, and friends. That's why Lincoln relied on it, and you can too.

Position Yourself for the Future

Shall we continue in sin, that grace may abound? God forbid. How shall we, that are dead to sin, live any longer therein?

Romans 6:1–2

> *Shall we go on to sin,*
> *Because thy grace abounds?*
> *Or crucify the Lord again,*
> *And open all his wounds?*
> *We will be slaves no more,*
> *Since Christ has made us free;*
> *Has nail'd our tyrants to his cross,*
> *And bought our liberty.*

Sometimes to survive a crisis, you have to focus on the
future, not the present. To help the nation survive the war,
Lincoln often reminded the country that the sacrifices being
made were for future generations. It was for the children, and
the children of their children, that the Union must be reunited.
Lincoln was right, of course. Because of the sacrifices made
during the Civil War, millions of Americans are free. More
than 150 years ago, Lincoln proclaimed, "The struggle of today
is not altogether for today—it is for a vast future also." All of
today's struggles are for a better tomorrow. Are you positioned
for the future?

Be Prepared to Sacrifice for God

Shall we continue in sin, that grace may abound? God forbid. How shall we, that are dead to sin, live any longer therein?

Romans 6:1–2

> *Shall we go on to sin,*
> *Because thy grace abounds?*
> *Or crucify the Lord again,*
> *And open all his wounds?*
> *We will be slaves no more,*
> *Since Christ has made us free;*
> *Has nail'd our tyrants to his cross,*
> *And bought our liberty.*

Lincoln knew he might not get to see the end of the Civil War. He knew the things he stood for might cause his ultimate demise. But that wasn't grounds for him to back down. He simply trusted God. He wrote, "I do not consider I have ever accomplished anything without God; and if it is his will that I must die by the hand of an assassin, I must be resigned. I must do my duty as I see it, and leave the rest with God." Be prepared to sacrifice in life. If the cause you live for is true, and if God has called you to it, then you have no option but to give up your life for it. Have you noticed that those men and women of the past who are most remembered are also the ones who sacrificed the most? Rely on God enough to give up your life to him and his purposes.

Strive to Finish

For we wrestle not against flesh and blood, but against principalities, against powers, against the rulers of the darkness of this world, against spiritual wickedness in high places.

Ephesians 6:12

From strength to strength go on,
Wrestle, and fight, and pray;
Tread all the powers of darkness down,
And win the well-fought day.

According to Lincoln, the ability to be successful depended largely on one's own determination and resolve. He encouraged the country to make every effort. He told the Union, "Let us strive on to finish the work we are in: to bind up the nation's wounds; to care for him who shall have borne the battle, and for his widow, and his orphan—to do all which may achieve and cherish a just and lasting peace among ourselves, and with all nations." Strive to finish the race. If you are absolutely resolved to make it to the end, you'll be surprised at how much you can accomplish. How many things were never achieved because someone quit too early? Like Lincoln, be resolved to run until the race is over.

Do Not Despair

Blessed is the man that endureth temptation: for when he is tried, he shall receive the crown of life, which the Lord hath promised to them that love him.

James 1:12

When aught shall tempt my soul to stray
From heavenly wisdom's narrow way,
To shun the precept's holy light,
Or quit my hold on Jesus' might,
May He who felt temptation's power
Still guard me in that dangerous hour.

Worry and fear ruled the hearts of the country during the Civil War. And it's no surprise, as almost everyone in the country was affected by the loss of loved ones and a total disruption of lifestyle. Lincoln was aware of the possibility of total despair and consoled the nation by saying, "Yet, under all circumstances, trusting to our Maker, and through his wisdom and beneficence, to the great body of our people, we will not despair, or despond." How did Lincoln suggest the country survive depression? He encouraged Americans to seek refuge in God. Through God's sovereign wisdom and goodness, life could be lived without giving up or giving in. Are you worried sick? Find refuge in God. You can cast your cares on him because he cares for you.

Believe in Your Destiny

The Lord knoweth how to deliver the godly out of temptations.

2 Peter 2:9

What though fierce and strong temptations
Press around thee on the way,
And thy sinful inclinations
Often cause thee great dismay!
Look to Jesus,
Thou through him shalt gain the day.

Abraham Lincoln believed the United States of America had been assigned a sovereign destiny. He once wrote, "I wish you a long life and prosperity individually, and pray that with the perpetuity of those institutions under which we have all so long lived and prospered . . . the glorious destiny of our country [be] established forever." Because Lincoln believed so strongly that God was on freedom's side, he could have the personal perseverance to see the country through. That is what gave Lincoln his strength. In the same way, you can believe God has a glorious purpose for you and your life. If you do, you too can find the confidence and strength to achieve your life's dreams. The power of purpose is awesome, and it can guide you through life as it did President Lincoln.

Make Honesty Your Goal

For I say, through the grace given unto me, to every man that is among you, not to think of himself more highly than he ought to think.

Romans 12:3

Lord, if thou thy grace impart,
Poor in spirit, meek in heart,
I shall, as my Saviour, be
Rooted in humility:
Pleas'd with all the Lord provides,
Wean'd from all the world besides.

When someone is described as being "ambitious," we usually think of that person as being aggressive, high-strung, or even pushy. These are all characteristics with which none of us wants to be associated. So how can we be ambitious but still maintain the respect of other people? For Abraham Lincoln, the answer was simple. He staked his future on integrity and believed that all other successes would follow in the footsteps of honesty. "Every man is said to have his peculiar ambition," said Lincoln. "Whether it be true or not, I can say for one that I have no other so great as that of being truly esteemed of my fellow men by rendering myself worthy of their esteem." Are you ambitiously pursuing integrity?

The Value of Action

Walk worthy of the vocation wherewith ye are called, with all lowliness and meekness, with longsuffering, forbearing one another in love.

Ephesians 4:1–2

Meekness, humility, and love,
Did through thy conduct shine;
Oh may my whole deportment prove
A copy, Lord, of thine.

Lincoln was a reflective man not often prone to impulsiveness. But when conditions warranted action, he was swift and decisive. He didn't ponder things so long as to lose an opportunity. The ability to take action was important to Lincoln. He viewed it as a defining characteristic, one that separated leaders from followers. "He who does *something* at the head of one regiment will eclipse him who does *nothing* at the head of a hundred," he told a Union soldier. Do you lose opportunities in life because you are afraid to make decisions? Sometimes the best action to take is simply to take action. Those who achieve the most are often the ones who aren't afraid to make decisions.

Extol Virtues

All of you be subject one to another, and be clothed with humility: for God resisteth the proud, and giveth grace to the humble.

1 Peter 5:5

> *Lord, for ever at thy side*
> *May my place and portion be;*
> *Strip me of the robe of pride;*
> *Clothe me with humility.*

Lincoln didn't criticize others very often. He was an encourager, and when he doled out compliments, he focused on virtues. He congratulated others for their honesty and uprightness. When is the last time you received a compliment for your integrity? Today's culture, rather than valuing virtues, values materialistic things. Lincoln once wrote to a solider, "I believe you to be a brave and skillful soldier, which, of course, I like. You have confidence in yourself, which is a valuable if not an indispensable quality. You are ambitious, which, within reasonable bounds, does good rather than harm." It is important to value others' intrinsic worth, their goodness and honor, rather than how much they own or their status in society.

On Rank and Title

Let nothing be done through strife or vainglory; but in lowliness of mind let each esteem other better than themselves.

Philippians 2:3

Oh, let each esteem his brother
Better than himself to be;
And let each prefer another,
Full of love, from envy free:
Happy are we,
When in this we all agree.

Today's culture places high value on a person's title and position, especially at work. President Lincoln was perturbed when officers begged for better rank. What mattered to Lincoln was not material reward, such as title or money, but instead that a person be respected and honored. Lincoln cared more about eternal rewards than earthly rewards. "Truth to speak, I do not appreciate this matter of rank on paper as you officers do," he wrote to an officer. "The world will not forget that you fought the battle of Stone River, but it will never care a fig whether you rank general on paper." Are you obsessed with your rank in life compared to other people? If so, maybe you ought to take Lincoln's approach. Let your promotion be in what others think of you, not what you tell others they ought to think of you.

Don't Betray Your Friends

Lest I should be exalted above measure through the abundance of the revelations, there was given to me a thorn in the flesh, the messenger of Satan to buffet me, lest I should be exalted above measure.

2 Corinthians 12:7

What though a thorn my bosom bears,
And varied are the wants and cares,
That mark my chequer'd way!
My God hath said, in whom I live,
"My grace is thine, and strength I give
According to thy day."

In Lincoln's view, disloyalty to a friend was paramount to treason. "I am willing to pledge myself in black and white to cut my own throat from ear to ear if, when I meet you, you shall *seriously* say that you believe me capable of betraying my friends for any price," he wrote to a rival politician. Lincoln didn't betray his friends for any reason. Sometimes in life we quit on our friends. They disappoint us in some way, or perhaps a quarrel separates us. Lincoln's loyalty to his friends was what made him popular. Do you think other people perceive you as a loyal friend? What do you do to develop and keep friends? If you lack companions and relationships in your life, maybe you ought to look at how loyal you've been. Let your friends know you're always there for them.

Surround Yourself with Integrity

Being confident of this very thing, that he which hath begun a good work in you will perform it until the day of Jesus Christ.

Philippians 1:6

He will complete the work begun,
He will his own defend;
Will give me strength my course to run,
And love me to the end.

Part of being honest and having integrity is surrounding yourself with those of like qualities. When elected president, Lincoln said, "In the formation of my cabinet, I shall aim as nearly as possible at perfection. Any man whom I may appoint to such a position must be, as far as possible, like Caesar's wife, pure and above suspicion, of unblemished reputation and undoubted integrity." Who do you associate with? People often are evaluated more by the friends they keep than by their own personal reputation. Abraham Lincoln knew this, and he made a point to associate with people who were respected, who had integrity and honor. Are your friends and associates respected? If not, that may be the reason you have trouble gaining respect yourself. It is important to find companions who will build up your reputation rather than destroy it.

Be Organized

His name shall endure for ever: his name shall be continued as long as the sun: and men shall be blessed in him: all nations shall call him blessed.

Psalm 72:17

Lord, let the thought of that bright day
Kindle our hopes, and warm our love;
Cheer us while here on earth we pray,
And crown our songs in heaven above.

Never claiming to be perfect, Lincoln admitted his mistakes. A general had sent an important letter, which Lincoln said he never received. He later remembered that he did receive the letter and admitted, "When I received the letter, I put it in my old hat and, buying a new one the next day, the old one was set aside; and so, the letter was lost sight of for a time." Most of the time Lincoln was organized, but this one time he admitted that he wasn't. Being organized might seem like a minor personal characteristic in comparison to values like honesty and integrity. But for Lincoln during the war, structure and organization were of equal importance. Virtues like honesty and integrity bring respect and admiration, but without an organized plan, it's hard to succeed.

Be Prudent

The time of my departure is at hand. I have fought a good fight, I have finished my course, I have kept the faith.

2 Timothy 4:6–7

Oh, most delightful hour by man
Experienced here below,
The hour that terminates his span
Of conflict and of woe!

"Make haste—slowly" was one of Lincoln's favorite proverbs, especially in regard to the war effort. Lincoln reminded his troops to be prudent. Move as quickly as possible, but not so fast as to make a near-sighted mistake. Take the long view, held Lincoln, but do it promptly. The secret in life is to find the balance between making haste and moving too slowly. Lincoln's point was that we should think before we act, avoiding spur-of-the-moment decisions.

Make Oaths You Can Keep

The God of peace shall bruise Satan under your feet shortly.

Romans 16:20

> *Now let my soul arise,*
> *And tread the tempter down;*
> *My Captain leads me forth*
> *To conquest and a crown:*
> *A feeble saint shall win the day,*
> *Though death and hell obstruct the way.*

Do you make promises you can't keep? Maybe that's because you're making too many of them. President Lincoln didn't make many promises. He knew a vow was too important a thing to make and then break, so he would make an oath only when he knew it was something he could live up to. Using the Bible to explain his philosophy, Lincoln once said to a friend who asked him to make a promise, "Remembering that Peter denied his Lord with an oath, after most solemnly protesting that he never would, I will not swear to make a committal." Lincoln looked to one of the most famous broken vows in history as an example of how even the most sincere vows can be broken under pressure. The next time you think about making a vow, first consider what it might take to keep it.

Promote Compromise

Thanks be to God, which giveth us the victory through our
Lord Jesus Christ.

1 Corinthians 15:57

Thus strong in the Redeemer's strength,
Sin, death, and hell we trample down,
Fight the good fight, and win at length,
Through mercy, an eternal crown.

As a lawyer, Abraham Lincoln actually discouraged his
clients from going to court. He preferred to settle a case without taking it before a judge and jury. "Discourage litigation.
Persuade your neighbors to compromise whenever you can,"
he counseled another lawyer. Lincoln was a reconciler. He pro-
moted compromise and cooperation, helping opposite sides
to try another view and to work out their differences. As a
young attorney, Lincoln became well-known in his community for avoiding trials. He didn't view his job as an adversary
as much as he did a counselor. As a result, his law practice flourished. People came to him because they knew he could help
figure out a way to save, not end, relationships. Are you eager
to help other people reconcile their differences?

Be Consistent

Who is among you that feareth the LORD, that obeyeth the voice of his servant, that walketh in darkness, and hath no light? let him trust in the name of the LORD, and stay upon his God.

Isaiah 1:10

If Providence our comforts shroud,
And dark distresses lower,
Hope paints its rainbow on the cloud,
And grace shines through the shower.

For Abraham Lincoln, values and ethics weren't something that changed with circumstances. The principles on which he campaigned were the same to which he held after he was elected to office. Once when a supporter asked Lincoln to consider changing his views on the slavery question, Lincoln replied, "It is desired that I shall shift the ground upon which I have been elected. I cannot do it. It would make me appear as if I repented for the crime of having been elected and was anxious to apologize and beg forgiveness." Do you ever find yourself compromising your convictions, even a little? Sometimes it is tempting to give up a principle in order to impress other people, to make you feel like you're a part of the crowd. Remember Lincoln's advice that being wishy-washy on your principles will ultimately make you look less dependable and trustworthy.

There's Hope in Eternity

The fear of man bringeth a snare: but whoso putteth his trust in the LORD shall be safe.

Proverbs 29:25

The taunts and frowns of men of earth,
What are they all to me!
Oh they are things of little worth,
Weigh'd with one smile from Thee,
Who bore a sorrow deeper far,
Than all these stingless trifles are.

Lincoln was known to have great compassion on the sick and terminally ill. When he comforted them, he would remind them of the ultimate promise—eternal life with Christ. In one letter to the spouse of a dying friend, he wrote, "If it be his lot to go now, he will soon have a joyous meeting with many loved ones gone before, and where the rest of us, through the help of God, hope ere long to join them." Having an eternal perspective makes life, and death, a lot easier. Lincoln knew that the end of life on earth only meant eternal joy with God. It was one of the principles that helped him lead the country through a dangerous and life-threatening time. Even if he died, he knew it wasn't the end of his life. If you can develop an eternal perspective, you'll find that almost everything in your life will become easier. There's hope for those who are prepared for eternity.

Be Bold

Trust in the LORD, and do good; so shalt thou dwell in the land, and verily thou shalt be fed.

Psalm 37:3–4

The birds without barn or store house are fed;
From them let us learn to trust for our bread:
His saints what is fitting shall ne'er be denied,
So long as 'tis written, The Lord will provide.

When Lincoln felt depressed and defeated, when the tide seemed to be turning against him, he looked not at his circumstances. Instead, he looked deep inside his own heart at the principles he knew to be true. He looked at the greatness of his cause and at God's will for his life. It was there that he found the power to proceed. He wrote in his journal, "If ever I feel the soul within me elevate and expand to those dimensions not wholly unworthy of its Almighty Architect, it is when I contemplate the cause of my country, deserted by the world beside, and I standing up boldly and alone and hurling defiance at her victorious oppressors." If your circumstances make you want to cry, don't look at them. Look deeper at those things in your life you know to be true. Look to God and his purposes for the strength to be bold.

Give a Second Chance

Thou, which hast shewed me great and sore troubles, shalt quicken me again, and shalt bring me up again from the depths of the earth.

Psalm 71:20

From every piercing sorrow
That heaves our breast to-day,
Or threatens us to-morrow,
Hope turns our eyes away;
On wings of faith ascending,
We see the land of light,
And feel our sorrows ending
In infinite delight.

Given the responsibility to decide the fate of a court-martialed soldier, would you be willing to give a second chance? As commander in chief, Lincoln was ultimately the one to decide whether or not a young soldier would live or die. Often the convicted soldier would not be much older than a child, not even eighteen years old. At the behest of some of his generals, Lincoln stood firm in his desire to give the younger men a second chance. "I am unwilling for any boy under eighteen to be shot," he demanded. These young men, according to Lincoln, deserved to learn a lesson by which to live, not die. Many of them ultimately became good husbands and fathers, and some of them even became great military leaders. Lincoln's forgiving attitude gave them the chance to begin again. Do you help other people start over, or are you eager to put an end to them?

Worship God

God is the strength of my heart, and my portion for ever.

Psalm 73:26

> *His boundless grace shall all my need supply,*
> *When streams of creature-comfort cease to flow:*
> *And should he some inferior good deny,*
> *'Tis but a greater blessing to bestow.*

Abraham Lincoln gained legendary status in America, becoming almost a godlike figure even before his assassination. While he was walking the streets of Richmond on April 4, 1865, a group of African American citizens ran to him, knelt at his feet, and thanked him for their newfound freedom. "Don't kneel to me," he said. "Kneel to God. I am but his humble instrument." Lincoln knew that it was only by God's grace and mercy that he was able to free the slaves. While other people looked to Lincoln, Lincoln looked to God. The Civil War was long and hard, and many times it was only through prayer that Lincoln gained the strength to continue. So when people attributed justice and freedom to him, he simply gave God the credit. Be careful not to take too much credit for your own victories when it was only by God's grace that you were able to achieve.

What to Do with Worry

God is our refuge and strength, a very present help in trouble. Therefore will not we fear, though the earth be removed, and though the mountains be carried into the midst of the sea.

Psalm 46:1–2

God is our refuge in distress,
A present help when dangers press;
In him undaunted I'll confide,
Though earth were from her centre toss'd,
And mountains in the ocean lost,
Torn piece-meal by the roaring tide.

What do you do with fear and worry? Lincoln had cause enough to worry, that's for sure. As the future of the country hung in the balance, the number of things to cause concern were innumerable. But he seemed to be at peace during much of the war. How did he handle the stress? After the Battle of Gettysburg, General Sickles asked Lincoln if he had been anxious and worried about the result. Lincoln replied, "No, I was not; some of my cabinet and many others in Washington were, but I had no fears. . . . God Almighty had taken the whole business into his own hands . . . and that is why I had no fears." Lincoln let God take his burdens, not worrying, but having faith. When he turned a matter over to God, he could forget about it and focus on things besides fear and worry. If Lincoln was able to turn over the Civil War to God, what do you think you can turn over to him?

Pray through Your Battles

Thou, O LORD, art a shield for me; my glory, and the lifter up of mine head.

Psalm 3:3

Lord, let thy grace surround me still,
And like a bulwark prove,
To guard my soul from every ill,
Secured by sovereign love.

After the Battle of Gettysburg, General James Rusling went to Lincoln about the battle at Vicksburg and asked for his thoughts. Rusling was concerned and wanted to know if Lincoln had any insight. "I have been praying for Vicksburg," Lincoln replied, "and I believe our heavenly Father is going to give us victory there too." Lincoln's reply startled General Rusling. He didn't expect Lincoln to talk about prayer and faith, but about military strategies. It was clear that Lincoln put as much trust in God as he did in his troops. He prayed through his battles. How do you get through battles in your life? Do you depend on your own strength or on the strength of God? If you follow Lincoln's lead, you can depend on a source greater than your own. You can put away worry and fear and concentrate on more important things. Pray through your battles!

Be Determined

Come unto me, all ye that labour and are heavy laden, and I will give you rest.

Matthew 11:28

> *Jesus, with thy word complying,*
> *Firm our faith and hope shall be;*
> *On thy faithfulness relying,*
> *We will seek our rest in thee.*

The Old Testament prophet Isaiah wrote, "They who wait for the LORD shall renew their strength, they shall mount up with wings like eagles, they shall run and not be weary, they shall walk and not faint" (Isa. 40:31 RSV). President Lincoln reminded the Union to do the same. "Let none falter who thinks he is right," he told Union soldiers during the depths of the Civil War. For Lincoln, the Union could be strong because of the rightness of its cause. It could persevere because it stood for the truth. How could evil win over good? How could injustice and bondage prevail? There's great strength in knowing you are right, and that alone can give you the strength to carry on. For those who worship God and wait upon him, there's no cause to falter. If God be for you, who can be against you?

Finish What You Start

I sink in deep mire, where there is no standing: I am come into deep waters, where the floods overflow me. I am weary of my crying: my throat is dried: mine eyes fail while I wait for my God.

Psalm 69:2–3

> *Prostrate before thy mercy-seat,*
> *I cannot if I would despair;*
> *None ever perish'd at thy feet,*
> *And I would lie for ever there.*

President Lincoln hesitated to take on a project until he knew he could finish it. He didn't want to say he would do something and then end up not doing it. He didn't oversell himself. In fact, he was prone to say very little about his plans until he was entirely confident that he could achieve them. "Before I resolve to do one thing or the other," he once said, "I must regain my confidence in my own ability to keep my resolves when they are made." When you take on something new, do you first count the cost? Or are you one of those people who has a lot of unfinished business? If you take Lincoln's approach, you'll become more trustworthy and reliable, because you'll be able to finish what you start. And you'll feel better about the things you say you'll do, because you'll know you can do them. The key to finishing what you start is to start only those things you know you can finish.

The Value of Determined Associates

Looking diligently lest any man fail of the grace of God; lest any root of bitterness springing up trouble you, and thereby many be defiled.

Hebrews 12:15

What bright exchange, what treasure shall be given,
For the lost birthright of a hope in heaven?
If lost the gem which empires could not buy,
What yet remains? —a dark eternity.

If you have a big task ahead of you, and you need some help, what qualities do you look for in people? Lincoln looked for people who were principled, grounded in the truth. "I hope those by whom I am surrounded have principles enough to nerve themselves for the task and leave nothing undone that can be fairly done to bring justice about the right result," he said.

Praying for Others

My beloved brethren, be ye stedfast, unmoveable, always abounding in the work of the Lord, forasmuch as ye know that your labour is not in vain in the Lord.

1 Corinthians 15:58

Sow in the morn thy seed,
At eve hold not thy hand,
To doubt and fear give thou no heed,
Broad-cast it round thy land.

Eliza Gurney was the widow of Joseph J. Gurney, an English Quaker and famed writer. Unlike many visitors to the White House, Eliza didn't come to pay her compliments. She came to pray with the president. Lincoln later recounted the event, saying she "uttered a short but most beautiful, eloquent, and comprehensive prayer that light and wisdom might be shed down from on high." Lincoln so treasured the prayer that he wrote her a letter. "In all, it has been your purpose to strengthen my reliance on God," he wrote, "and I am much indebted to the good Christian people of the country for their constant prayers and consolations; and to no one of them, more than to yourself." It wasn't very often that a citizen came to pray with the president, but in fact, that's what he would have liked. Take time to pray with another.

I Will

I know whom I have believed, and am persuaded that he is able to keep that which I have committed unto him against that day.

2 Timothy 1:12

Beneath his smiles my heart has liv'd,
And part of heaven possess'd;
I thank him for the grace receiv'd,
And trust him for the rest.

Once when giving an order to one of his generals, Lincoln received a reply he didn't like. The general started to say, "If I can . . . ," and was sternly interrupted by the president. "By all means, don't say, 'If I can'! Say, 'I will!'" For Lincoln, success was not an "iffy" matter. Lincoln knew that success came only to those with perseverance and willpower. As freedom and justice hung in the balance, there was no room in Lincoln's vocabulary for "if." He had to win the war, and anyone who didn't share his tenacity was disregarded. How is your perseverance? Are your plans contingent upon "ifs" and "buts"? If so, take Lincoln's approach and tell yourself—and others—that you will achieve your plans.

Faith Makes Might

Whatsoever thy hand findeth to do, do it with thy might; for there is no work, nor device, nor knowledge, nor wisdom, in the grave, whither thou goest.

Ecclesiastes 9:10

Whate'er our hands shall find to do,
To-day may we with zeal pursue;
Seize fleeting moments as they fly,
And live as we would wish to die.

"Let us have faith that right makes might; and in that faith let us, to the end, dare to do our duty as we understand," encouraged Lincoln. For President Lincoln, the war would be won not on military prowess, but on faith. Lincoln believed that truth would prevail. He believed in the biblical portent that the Union's faith would heal the country. Do you have the faith to endure? Like Lincoln, you may not feel like you have the resources to persevere. You may feel like you're sure to lose. For Lincoln, though, all that really mattered was to have faith. The most important thing was to believe.

The Great Counselor

Beloved, let us love one another: for love is of God; and every one that loveth is born of God, and knoweth God.

1 John 4:7

Bless'd be the tie that binds
Our hearts in Christian love;
The fellowship of kindred minds
Is like to that above.

After Jesus' death and resurrection, he promised to send his disciples a helper, the Holy Spirit. Abraham Lincoln was the first and only American president to call upon the Holy Spirit publicly. On July 15, 1863, Lincoln wrote to the American people, "I invite the people of the United States to invoke the influence of His Holy Spirit . . . to guide the counsels of the government with wisdom adequate to so great a national emergency, and to visit with tender care and consolation throughout the length and breadth of our land all those who, through the vicissitudes of marches, voyages, battles, and sieges, have been brought to suffer in mind, body, or estate." Lincoln asked the Holy Spirit to give divine wisdom and knowledge and to help console the afflicted. Lincoln leaned not only on a "higher power," but named God's only Son, Jesus, and the Holy Spirit.

An Honest Man Comes Clean

Walk in love, as Christ also hath loved us, and hath given himself for us an offering and a sacrifice to God for a sweetsmelling savour.

Ephesians 5:2

Among the saints on earth
Let mutual love be found;
Heirs of the same inheritance,
With mutual blessings crown'd.

One of the oddest letters ever received by President Abraham Lincoln was sent anonymously. It contained $860 and an apology. The sender apparently had stolen the money from the government. "Being tempted, in an unguarded moment," he wrote, "I consented to take it being very much in want of money, but thanks be to my Savior, I was led by the influences of the Holy Spirit to see my great sin and to return it to you as the representative of the United States." Lincoln's reputation for being an honest representative of the United States of America loomed so large, this particular person felt responsible to do good in his sight. The better your reputation, the better people will act before you.

Thank God for Your Blessings

Speak not evil one of another, brethren. He that speaketh evil of his brother, and judgeth his brother, speaketh evil of the law, and judgeth the law: but if thou judge the law, thou art not a doer of the law, but a judge.

James 4:11

> *Love is pure and heavenly flame,*
> *And much regards a brother's name;*
> *It hopeth all things, and believes,*
> *Nor easily a charge receives.*

A Bible discovered at the Fisk University Library in Nashville, Tennessee, is inscribed: "To Abraham Lincoln. . . . We present to you this copy of the Holy Scriptures, as a token of respect for your active participation in furtherance of the cause of the emancipation of our race. This great event will be a matter of history. Hereafter, when our children shall ask what mean these tokens, they will be told of your worthy deeds, and will rise up and call you blessed. . . . May the King Eternal, an all-wise Providence protect and keep you, and when you pass from this world to that of eternity, may you be borne to the bosom of your Savior and your God." Those who presented this Bible to President Lincoln had thankful hearts. By giving Lincoln a Bible, they recognized not only Lincoln, but God as well. They were thankful that God worked through Lincoln to secure their freedom. With a grateful heart, give thanks to God.

A Must Attitude

Praying always with all prayer and supplication in the Spirit
. . . and for me, that utterance may be given unto me, that I
may open my mouth boldly, to make known the mystery of
the gospel.

Ephesians 6:18–19

With heavenly power, O Lord, defend
Those whom we now to thee commend;
Thy faithful messengers secure,
And make them to the end endure.

Lincoln was tenacious and unyielding. He believed victory
was handed to those who had the most desire to win. Once a
young colonel came to him for advice. "Having made the
attempt," he said, "you must succeed in it." *Must* is the opera-
tive word here. "I know not how to aid you save in the assurance of one of mature age," he continued, "and much severe
experience, that you *can* not fail if you resolutely determine
that you *will* not." Do you have a *must* attitude? President
Lincoln knew the stakes were high during the Civil War. Freedom and justice hung in the balance, and the lives of hundreds of thousands of men, women, and children were at stake.
What if Lincoln expressed to the Union that they *might* win
the war? What if he merely told them, it was *possible?* How
do you look at your life and the things you want to accomplish? Have Lincoln's attitude. You *must.*

Look at All Your Alternatives

If ye fulfil the royal law according to the scripture, Thou shalt love thy neighbour as thyself, ye do well.

James 2:8

Love lays its own advantage by
To seek its neighbour's good;
So God's own Son came down to die,
And bought our lives with blood.

Love is the grace that keeps its power,
In all the realms above;
There faith and hope are known no more
But saints for ever love.

Before quitting do you try every possibility? Do you look at all your options? "I shall not surrender this game leaving any available card unplayed," said Lincoln to his dog-tired generals. Look at all your alternatives before surrendering. Sometimes the last card played wins the match. It's easy to be dissuaded when you're down, when you think you've lost. But no matter how far behind, you never know your chances until you take them all. Lincoln could have quit early in the war. He could have compromised and negotiated a settlement. Instead, he instructed his generals to look for other alternatives. He told them to be creative and seek out hidden, yet-to-be-seen ways to defeat the Confederacy. Is that what you do when you're behind? For anyone who's ever come from behind to win, has there ever been any other way? Be sure to look at all your alternatives.

Don't Be Discouraged

Let every one of us please his neighbour for his good to edification.

Romans 15:2

May I from every act abstain,
That hurts or gives another pain:
Still may I feel my heart inclin'd
To be the friend of all mankind.

The Civil War was a confusing time. Not only was the country at war, but it was at war with itself. Relationships were strained between families and friends. Finances were tight, even nonexistent, for most people. There was much loneliness and despair as disease and death spread throughout the country. Nevertheless, Lincoln calmly told the citizens of the Union, "Let nothing discourage or baffle you." He told them to be clear-minded, not to be disoriented, but to stay focused on the absolute rightness of what they were doing. There are times in life when things do seem confused, when everything that was familiar and in order suddenly becomes disorderly. At times like these, look to the One who is good and true, then heed Lincoln's advice and don't be baffled.

Use God's Word

The Lord make you to increase and abound in love one toward another, and toward all men, even as we do toward you.

1 Thessalonians 3:12

May love, that shining grace,
O'er all my powers preside;
Direct my thoughts, suggest my words,
And every action guide.

President Abraham Lincoln often went to the Bible for wisdom. Once an opposing political candidate asked Lincoln to say he was sorry for the position he took on the slavery issue. Lincoln knew he was right and refused to apologize. He replied to his opponent with a scriptural illustration. "Repentance before forgiveness is a provision of the Christian system," he told a crowd, "and on that condition alone will the Republicans grant forgiveness." Lincoln's response silenced his critics. Do you refer to God's Word only in church or only when you're praying, or do you live it every day? Lincoln used the Bible to support a view he knew was right. He leaned on God's Word not only in his private devotional time, but as an instrument to live by, day after day. He wasn't afraid to speak God's words, because he knew the truthfulness of Scripture would speak louder than anything else he might say.

The Hard Path of Duty

Whosoever believeth that Jesus is the Christ is born of God.

1 John 5:1

Lord, I believe thy heavenly word;
Fain would I have my soul renew'd;
I mourn for sin, and trust the Lord
To have it pardon'd and subdued.

O may thy grace its power display,
Let guilt and death no longer reign;
Save me in thine appointed way,
Nor let my humble faith be vain.

Once Abraham Lincoln was asked the best advice to give a young person. Lincoln looked to his own life, remembered how hard he had worked as a young frontiersman, and said, "It is *much* for the young to know that treading the hard path of duty . . . *will* be noticed and *will* lead to high places." Lincoln talked much about the "hard path of duty." It meant not only working hard, but working hard for the right things. It meant working hard to help others, to support your family, to live a life of integrity, no matter how hard it might be at times. For Lincoln, being ambitious, achieving things, and acquiring material wealth wasn't enough. The "hard path of duty" meant to be responsible and do what you had to do, not just what you felt like doing. That was not only the way a frontiersman survived, but how all men and women survive.

Actions Speak Louder Than Words

Whosoever shall confess that Jesus is the Son of God, God dwelleth in him, and he in God.

1 John 4:15

I'll tell to all poor sinners round,
How great a Saviour I have found;
I'll point to his redeeming blood,
And say, "Behold the way to God."

Have you ever known a person who said very little but worked very hard? These kind of people are generally well liked and successful. Lincoln was known for his great oratorical skills. People would come from many miles just to hear him speak. But Lincoln himself did not consider articulate and moving speech as an indication of a successful person. "Many eloquent men fail utterly. . . . They are not, as a class, generally successful." What did Lincoln mean? Simply put, actions speak louder than words. We all know people who talk a lot but say little and act even less. What's important in life is not what you say but what you do. No one is remembered just for his or her words, especially if they were not acted upon. So if you're going to gain the trust of others, just work hard.

Be Responsible

For whether we live, we live unto the Lord; and whether we die, we die unto the Lord: whether we live therefore, or die, we are the Lord's.

Romans 14:8

> *My soul, and all its powers,*
>   *Thine, wholly thine, shall be;*
> *All, all my happy hours*
>   *I consecrate to thee:*
> *Whate'er I have, whate'er I am,*
>   *Shall magnify my Saviour's name.*

The decision to emancipate the slaves was one of the most controversial decisions made by a president in America's history. Making the decision without an act of Congress, Lincoln himself bore the responsibility. Later Lincoln was asked how he was able to make such a monumental decision. "What I did," he said, "I did after very full deliberation and under a very heavy and solemn sense of responsibility. I can only trust in God I have made no mistake." Lincoln knew the largeness of his task, and he refused to think he could take it on by himself. He said he could "only" trust God. Giving God the responsibility did two things. First, it gave Lincoln the confidence to make the decision and to live by it. Second, it gave the American people the confidence that the decision wasn't made by man alone. On the contrary, it was made by the Almighty. If you trust God with your decisions, you and those who live with you can be at peace.

Ask for God's Favor First

For I have given you an example, that ye should do as I have done to you.

John 13:15

Thy fair example may I trace,
To teach me what I ought to be:
Make me, by thy transforming grace,
My Saviour, daily more like thee.

When Lincoln plunged into war against the Confederacy, he asked not only for the support of his country, but for God's favor. Do you remember to ask for God's favor? The next time you find yourself in a bind, between a rock and a hard place, take the words of Lincoln as he too started something he knew was going to be hard. "Upon this act," he wrote, "sincerely believed to be an act of justice, warranted by the Constitution, upon military necessity, I invoke the considerable judgment of mankind, and the gracious favor of Almighty God." Asking for God's mercy, wisdom, and goodwill isn't just an extra step; it's the first step.

Strive for Perfection

Behold, I lay in Zion a chief corner stone, elect, precious: and he that believeth on him shall not be confounded. Unto you therefore which believe he is precious.

1 Peter 2:6–7

> *Jesus, in thy transporting name*
> *What glories meet our eyes!*
> *Thou art the angels' sweetest theme,*
> *The wonder of the skies.*
>
> *Oh may our willing hearts confess*
> *Thy sweet, thy gentle sway;*
> *Glad captives of thy matchless grace,*
> *Thy righteous rule obey.*

Abraham Lincoln was the kind of man who was always reaching for a higher plane. He wasn't satisfied with his present self, but always strove to improve his condition. He worked hard on himself, physically, mentally, and spiritually. Where did he get his tenacious self-improvement habits? He gave a hint when he wrote, "The Saviour, I suppose, did not expect that any human creature could be perfect as the Father in heaven; but He said, 'As your Father in Heaven is perfect, be ye also perfect.' He set that up as a standard, and He who did most towards reaching that standard attained to the highest degree of moral perfection." Like Lincoln, we ought to look to the words of Jesus, who taught that we should be the best we can be. Those who strive to be perfect, although they may not arrive there, are sure to be more ideal than those who don't.

Admit Your Mistakes

Ye are not in the flesh, but in the Spirit, if so be that the Spirit of God dwell in you. Now if any man have not the Spirit of Christ, he is none of his.

Romans 8:9

Author of our new creation,
   Let us all thine influence prove;
Make our souls thy habitation;
   Shed abroad the Saviour's love.

How many times have you held your ground, even when you knew you were wrong? It's hard to admit when you're wrong, but we all respect those who do. Lincoln was quick to admit his mistakes and errors. He didn't like for anyone to think he was being dishonest or fraudulent. So anytime he was proven wrong, he immediately confessed. "Holding it a sound maxim that it is better to be only sometimes right than at all times wrong," he said, "so soon as I discover my opinions to be erroneous I shall be ready to renounce them." The secret to being able to admit your mistakes is to do it soon. The longer it goes, the harder it gets. That's why Lincoln said "so soon as I discover. . . ."

Do unto Others, Even Adversaries

The righteous shall hold on his way, and he that hath clean hands shall be stronger and stronger.

Job 17:9

The righteous, bless'd with light divine,
Shall prosper on their way;
Brighter and brighter still shall shine,
To glory's perfect day.

It's easy to deal with friends in a kindhearted manner. It's easy to forgive a friend. But for those whom you don't like— your enemies—it's a little harder. According to Lincoln, though, it's all the same. "I don't want to be unjustly accused of dealing illiberally or unfairly with an adversary, either in court or in a political canvass or anywhere else," he said. "I would despise myself if I supposed myself ready to deal less liberally with an adversary than I was willing to be treated myself." The issue is not friend or enemy. It's about you and how you would like to be treated. To live by the golden rule, sometimes you have to put yourself in your enemy's shoes. Look at things from your enemy's perspective. Then treat him or her as you would want to be treated.

Get Your Facts Straight

Dearly beloved, avenge not yourselves, but rather give place unto wrath: for it is written, Vengeance is mine; I will repay, saith the Lord.

Romans 12:19

May I feel beneath my wrongs
Vengeance to the Lord belongs;
Nor a worse requital dare,
Than the meek revenge of prayer:
Much forgiven, may I learn,
Love for hatred to return.

Before taking action on the views or opinions of others, it's always a good idea to find some evidence. You can't always rely on what someone else says. Lincoln learned this during the war. After listening too closely to another man's judgment and making a mistake, he decided, "We better know there is fire whence we see much smoke rising than [we] could know it by one or two witnesses swearing to it. The witnesses may commit perjury, but the smoke cannot." Lincoln looked hard and long for answers to his questions, trying to learn the whole story and not just one side of it. Do you make hasty decisions before you learn the whole story, and later regret it? Take Lincoln's advice and look for the smoke before trying to put out the fire.

How to Find Evil

Keep thy heart with all diligence; for out of it are the issues of life.

Proverbs 4:23

> *Thy business be to keep thy heart,*
> *Each passion to control;*
> *Nobly ambitious well to rule*
> *The empire of thy soul.*

Lincoln often paraphrased Scripture when trying to make a point. Once a Union general made a misstep, and Lincoln began to mistrust not only the man's judgment, but his motives as well. But as he talked through the situation with others and noticed that the general led an honest life, he paraphrased what Jesus said about good and evil in the Gospel of Matthew: "An *evil* tree cannot bring forth *good* fruit." Do you rely on Jesus' words to help you determine the motives of others? Lincoln knew that God could best help him evaluate this man's heart. Using the Bible's advice, he looked at the fruit of this man's life. He knew that's where he could find the truth. The next time you're faced with a similar situation, look at the fruit and remember that's what counts the most.

Remember Your Mortality

Take heed to yourselves, lest at any time your hearts be over-charged with surfeiting, and drunkenness, and cares of this life, and so that day come upon you unawares.

Luke 21:34

> *The world employs its various snares,*
> *Of hopes and pleasures, pains and cares,*
> *And chain'd to earth I lie:*
> *When shall my fetter'd powers be free,*
> *And leave these seats of vanity,*
> *And upward learn to fly?*

Even at the height of his success as president and commander in chief, Lincoln never forgot his mortality. He wasn't fooled, like some successful men and women, into thinking he was a god. "We all *know* that we have to die," he once wrote. "We know it because we know, or at least we think we know, that of all the beings just like ourselves who have been coming into the world for six thousand years, not one is now living who was here two hundred years ago." Lincoln was well aware of his humanity, which was one of the reasons he was able to stay level-headed and make sound decisions. He knew there would be an end for him, that his fate was sealed just like that of everyone else. It was what kept him humble. And his humility is what made him great. Remember your mortality.

The Bible Is Relevant

In all things showing thyself a pattern of good works: in doctrine shewing uncorruptness, gravity, sincerity.

Titus 2:7

Pure may I be, averse to sin,
Just, holy, merciful, and true;
And let thine image form'd within,
Shine out in all I speak or do.

President Lincoln, a devoted Bible reader, claimed that the Bible helped move him to issue the Emancipation Proclamation, freeing America's slaves, in 1863. When making his decision, he looked to the history of the Jews, who were enslaved in Egypt. He likened the situation to when Moses asked Pharaoh to let God's people go. Lincoln especially noted the words in Exodus 6:5: "I [God] have also heard the groaning of the children of Israel, whom the Egyptians keep in bondage." Lincoln often looked to God's Word for help in making decisions. He took examples from the Bible and applied them to his daily life. The Word of God was relevant for Lincoln, and it can be relevant in your life too.

Morality Secures Your Future

Blessed are those servants, whom the lord when he cometh shall find watching: verily I say unto you, that he shall gird himself, and make them to sit down to meat, and will come forth and serve them.

Luke 12:37

Arm me with jealous care,
As in thy sight to live:
And oh, thy servant, Lord, prepare,
A strict account to give.

Help me to watch and pray,
And on thyself rely;
Assured if I my trust betray,
I shall for ever die.

"The only assurance of our nation's safety is to lay our foundation in morality and religion," wrote President Lincoln. Lincoln often remarked about the importance of morality. And he believed that without religion and the Bible, there could be no real morality. The moral framework that held the nation together rested on the foundation of the Christian religion, in things like prayer and faith. Without these things, Lincoln knew the country would not stand. Likewise, for each individual, morality and religion play an important role. They are the things that secure your future and keep you safe from ruining your life. The only assurance of your safety is to lay your foundation in morality and religion.

Judge Not

Take heed, brethren, lest there be in any of you an evil heart of unbelief, in departing from the living God.

Hebrews 3:12

How oft, deceived by self and pride,
Has my weak heart been turn'd aside;
And, Jonah-like, has fled from thee,
Till thou hast look'd again on me!

Abraham Lincoln used biblical lessons once when his wife, Mary, scolded him for not being tough enough on the Confederacy. She told him he was too sympathetic and compassionate. She wanted swift and strict punishment. Lincoln retorted, quietly but sternly, with the words of Jesus, "Judge not, lest ye be judged." Lincoln was not so confident in the goodness of the Union as to think he could pass judgment on those who didn't agree. He knew his own faults, how the Union had let God down in many other ways too. He wasn't about to treat the Confederacy as if he were perfect, so he leaned on the Bible's advice to let God do the judging. Are you quick to judge? Or is someone telling you to be a stronger judge? The best advice is Lincoln's. Let God do the judging.

On Greed

Thou hast dealt well with thy servant, Oh LORD, according unto thy word.

Psalm 119:65

> *Since first the maze of life I trod,*
> *Hast thou not hedged about my way,*
> *My worldly vain designs withstood,*
> *And robb'd my passions of their prey?*
> *Thrice happy loss, which makes me see*
> *My happiness alone in thee!*

President Lincoln once warned America not to be too self-indulgent. As the country grew and began to prosper, he noticed less moderation and more greed. Materialism prevailed over generosity. Abraham Lincoln believed America had grown too proud as it flourished. "We have been the recipients of the choicest bounties of Heaven. We have been preserved, these many years, in peace and prosperity. We have grown in numbers, wealth, and power as no other nation has ever grown; but we have forgotten God," he wrote. Those words could as easily be written today as in 1864. The more we get, the more we covet. The more we acquire, the less of God we think we need.

Too Proud to Pray

We have had fathers of our flesh which corrected us, and we gave them reverence: shall we not much rather be in subjection unto the Father of spirits, and live?

Hebrews 12:9

> *Oh let my trembling soul be still,*
> *While darkness veils this mortal eye,*
> *And wait thy wise, thy holy will*
> *Wrapp'd yet in tears and mystery:*
> *I cannot, Lord, thy purpose see,*
> *Yet all is well — since ruled by thee.*

They say success breeds success. But sometimes too much success breeds feelings of self-sufficiency and self-reliance. Instead of relying on God, our success can make us feel independent of God and we begin to rely on our own strength. Abraham Lincoln warned, "Intoxicated with unbroken success, we have become too self-sufficient to feel the necessity of redeeming and preserving grace, too proud to pray to the God who made us." Lincoln knew who is sovereign. There is no such thing as an independent person. All are reliant on God, and those who become too proud to pray are often the first to fall.

Pray for God's Mercy

Put them in mind to be subject to principalities and powers, to obey magistrates, to be ready to every good work.

Titus 3:1

> *Lord, thou hast bid thy people pray*
> *For all that bear the sovereign sway,*
> *Who as thy servants reign;*
> *Rulers, and governors, and powers —*
> *Behold, in faith we pray for ours;*
> *Nor let us plead in vain.*

"And whereas, when our own beloved country, once, by the blessing of God, united, prosperous, and happy, is now afflicted with faction and civil war, it is peculiarly fit for us to recognize the hand of God in this terrible visitation, and in sorrowful remembrance of our own faults and crimes as a nation and as individuals, to humble ourselves before Him, and to pray for His mercy." When you pray, do you ask for God's mercy? Many times we ask for God's favor, or we ask for God to help solve a problem. But it's probably not very often we ask for his mercy. Instead of asking God to give him victory, Lincoln begged for God's mercy. He wanted God's grace to forgive, not his power to win. Pray for God's mercy.

On Intolerance

Wherefore, beloved, seeing that ye look for such things, be diligent that ye may be found of him in peace, without spot, and blameless.

2 Peter 3:14

Yet with these prospects full in sight
I'll wait thy signal for my flight;
For while thy service I pursue,
I find a heaven in all I do.

Lincoln was probably tempted to compromise many times during the Civil War, to negotiate a deal that would bring an end to the bloodshed. He could have brought a quick and peaceful resolution to the crisis by just giving in to some of the demands of the South. But to Lincoln, the eternal cause of freedom and equality were preeminently more important than temporal peace. "Often a limb must be amputated to save a life; but a life is never wisely given to save a limb," he wrote. Lincoln wouldn't tolerate anything but a permanent and lasting solution—freedom and liberty for all. There are times in life when it's tempting to give in, to find a pleasant means to an end. When you're tempted to compromise, remember Lincoln. Don't cut off your life to save a limb.

Don't Be Afraid to Fail

Ye were the servants of sin, but ye have obeyed from the heart that form of doctrine which was delivered you. Being then made free from sin, ye became the servants of righteousness.

Romans 6:17–18

Love is the fountain whence
All true obedience flows;
The Christian serves the God he loves,
And loves the God he knows.

One reason Abraham Lincoln succeeded in life was because he wasn't afraid to fail. In fact, failure was the key to his success. Why? Because he looked upon failure as a learning experience. He may have been disappointed when he failed, but he didn't let it stop him. Failure was his schoolhouse. Ever since Lincoln was a boy, he was accustomed to bearing the brunt of life's failures and disappointments. Life often didn't go his way. But at every turn of events, good or bad, Lincoln would observe what happened, make mental notes, and move on. Newspaper publisher Horace Greeley once said of Lincoln, "He slowly won his way to eminence and fame doing the work that lay next to him—doing it with all his growing might—doing it as well as he could, and learning by his failure, when failure was encountered, how to do it better."

Failure Is the Best Teacher

I will delight myself in thy commandments, which I have loved.

Psalm 119:47

Then shall my heart have inward joy,
And keep my face from shame,
When all thy statutes I obey,
And honour all thy name.

Lincoln was known to admit his faults and failures. He had, in fact, failed on many occasions. He lost no less than seven political campaigns before being elected president of the United States. But Lincoln looked at failure differently than most other people do. He used failure as a lesson. He learned from it rather than let it get him down. Once when speaking to a group of young people, Lincoln said, "I find quite as much material for a lecture in those points wherein I have failed as in those wherein I have been moderately successful." Lincoln learned early in life that things go wrong. Life isn't always as we might have planned or wanted it to be. Lincoln looked past that and let life's failures and disappointments be his teachers. If we all had the same inclination, there's no telling what we might achieve.

Have Faith in Yourself

Ye did run well; who did hinder you, that ye should not obey the truth?

Galatians 5:7

> *Better that we had never known*
> *The way to heaven through saving grace,*
> *Than basely in our lives disown,*
> *And slight and mock thee to thy face.*

How would you feel if your life were open to a full public investigation? For most people, that might be an embarrassing and uneasy situation. But if you live a transparent life, full of integrity, it wouldn't be that hard. "I never despair of sustaining myself before the people upon any measure that will stand a full investigation," said Lincoln. He was honest with himself and others. He lived an upright life and quickly admitted his wrongdoings. As such, he didn't have to worry that he might be "found out" someday. You can have faith in yourself and trust yourself if you do like Lincoln and simply be honest when you're good and when you're not so good.

Stand Firm

This God is our God for ever and ever: he will be our guide even unto death.

Psalm 48:14

Haste thee on from grace to glory,
Arm'd by faith, and wing'd by prayer;
Heaven's eternal day's before thee,
God's own hand shall guide thee there.

Abraham Lincoln knew the secret to winning. He knew the surefire way to victory anytime and anywhere. "We shall not fail," he said. "If we stand firm, we shall not fail." Lincoln's secret was to stand firm. That meant not backing down, holding one's ground and not quitting. Most people do quit too early. They give up in the face of failure. They don't persevere. Lincoln knew that all it took to win in any given situation was to be the last person standing. So he simply stood firm. How many times might you have won something if you had waited just a little longer? Sometimes all winning in life takes is to be a little more patient and enduring. If you stand firm long enough, you're bound to be the last person standing.

Let God Set Things Right

Then Samuel took a stone, and set it between Mizpeh and Shen, and called the name of it Ebenezer, saying, Hitherto hath the LORD helped us.

1 Samuel 7:12

Here I raise my Ebenezer,
Hither, by thy help, I'm come:
And I hope, by thy good pleasure,
Safely to arrive at home.

Everyone experiences trials and tribulations now and then. When your horizons look a little cloudy, where do you look for help? Lincoln's horizons were more than just cloudy. As the storm clouds of war surrounded him, as he lost a son to disease, and as his friends turned against him, he found himself in a hurricane. Nevertheless, he was assured that all things would work together for good. God would make things right. "The political horizon looks dark and lowering," he said, "but the people, under Providence, will set all right." For Lincoln, Providence was the God of the Bible. He believed that because of the prayers of the people, God would take them through the storm to safer waters. And God can take you through your storms if you go to him in prayer.

Respect the Opinions of Older Generations

Who am I, O Lord GOD? and what is my house, that thou hast brought me hitherto? and this was yet a small thing in thy sight, O Lord GOD.

2 Samuel 7:18–19

> *Render'd safe by his protection,*
> *I shall pass the watery waste;*
> *Trusting to his wise direction,*
> *I shall gain the port at last;*
> *And with wonder,*
> *Think on toils and dangers past.*

Where do you go for help when you need good advice? Lincoln went to the aged, the more mature and seasoned people. "I love the sentiments of those old-time men and shall be most happy to abide by their opinions." It may not always be the most common or popular place to go, but sometimes you'll find the best advice from those who have experienced the most in life—the older generation.

Don't Neglect Your Friends

It is of the Lord's mercies that we are not consumed, because his compassions fail not. They are new every morning: great is thy faithfulness.

Lamentations 3:22–23

> *Lift up to God the voice of praise,*
> *Whose goodness, passing thought,*
> *Loads every minute as it flies*
> *With benefits unsought.*

Lincoln was known throughout his life for his loyalty to his friends. He never forgot them. "Our friends are too numerous to be named individually, yet each of them is too dear to be forgotten or neglected," he once quipped. Because Lincoln was so loyal to his friends, he had many of them. Do you lack friendships? What do you do to keep your friends? Try taking Lincoln's advice: Don't neglect your friends, and they won't neglect you.

Be an Entrepreneur

He hath not dealt with us after our sins; nor rewarded us according to our iniquities.

Psalm 103:10

He hath with a piteous eye
Look'd upon our misery:
Let us, then, with gladsome mind,
Praise the Lord, for he is kind:
For his mercies shall endure,
Ever faithful, ever sure.

Abraham Lincoln aimed to go where no man had gone before. "Towering genius disdains a beaten path," he wrote. He didn't like to do things the way people expected him to do them. He forged new frontiers, took paths not often taken. And it took him from frontiersman to president. If you want to find extraordinary success in life, you can't travel down the same path as everyone else. You have to make a new way to find a new place. If there was one thing that separated Abraham Lincoln from others, it was his unique, almost unpredictable, approach to life. He was a entrepreneur.

Take Refuge in God

The fruit of the Spirit is love, joy, peace, longsuffering, gentleness, goodness, faith, meekness, temperance: against such there is no law.

Galatians 5:22–23

'Tis God himself the ground prepares,
His Spirit sows the land;
And every pleasant fruit it bears,
Is nurtur'd by his hand.

Once Abraham Lincoln was called to the side of a young, dying soldier. Comforting the young man was most assuredly a hard thing to do. Words don't come easily. Lincoln didn't have many words to give, but what he said made all the difference. "He notes the fall of a sparrow and numbers the hair of our heads; and He will not forget the dying man who puts his trust in him," he said, paraphrasing the Bible. That's all that needed to be said. For when you believe in a God who cares for the birds of the air, there's no need to worry about what's going to happen to you. We don't know much more about this dying soldier, but we do know his circumstance was much like we'll all face someday. When we do, let's remember the words of Abraham Lincoln. If we put our trust in God, there's no cause for concern.

Call upon the Name of the Lord

Let no corrupt communication proceed out of your mouth, but that which is good to the use of edifying, that it may minister grace unto the hearers.

Ephesians 4:29

Wheresoever two or three
Meet, a Christian company,
Grant us, Lord, to meet with thee:
Gracious Saviour, hear!
When with friends beloved we stray,
Talking down the closing day,
Saviour, meet us in the way:
Gracious Saviour, hear!

"Call upon and confide in our great and good and merciful Maker, who will not turn away . . . in any extremity," Abraham Lincoln wrote. Why did he call on the name of the Lord? He called on God because he believed God was great enough to help, good enough to want to help, and benevolent enough to answer his prayers. Lincoln called on God because he trusted that God was on his side and that he was able, ready, and willing to help. Lincoln was so confident in God, he told the nation to call upon his name "in any extremity." It makes no difference how difficult the situation, God is there to help. If Lincoln, who faced war and death, could call upon the name of the Lord, then why not you and I during our trials?

Encourage

Let your light so shine before men, that they may see your good works, and glorify your Father which is in heaven.

Matthew 5:16

So let our lips and lives express
The holy gospel we profess;
So let our works and virtues shine
To prove the doctrine all divine.

Sometimes when a friend is down, when someone close to you is ready to give in, you need to do what Lincoln once did. A Union general was dog-tired and ready to resign. He told Lincoln in a letter that he couldn't go on. Lincoln did what any good friend ought to do. He encouraged him and told him to hold on. "I have seen your dispatch expressing your unwillingness to break your hold where you are," he wrote the general. ". . . Hold on with a bulldog grip, and chew and choke as much as possible." By giving the general a positive push, Lincoln gave him the internal strength to want to carry on. When those around you say they want to quit, do you spur them on or help them stop? Learn to encourage like Lincoln. Learn to help your friends "hold on with a bulldog grip."

Happiness Is a Choice

That ye may be blameless and harmless, the sons of God, without rebuke, in the midst of a crooked and perverse nation, among whom ye shine as lights in the world.

Philippians 2:15

That wisdom, Lord, on us bestow
From every evil to depart,
To stop the mouth of every foe,
While upright both in life and heart,
The proof of godly fear we give,
And show them how the Christians live.

Are you happy to see other people happy? Sometimes when our own lives aren't going so well, we tend to be jealous of those who are living through better times. Lincoln liked to see other people happy, no matter his own circumstances. "Nothing would make me more miserable than to believe you miserable," he said to a friend, "and nothing more happy than to know you were so." This is an important lesson to learn but not always easy. To want to see other people doing well is a choice we have to make. Lincoln did, and others loved him for it. If your attitude is the same, if your aim in life is to make others happy, you might find yourself as popular as Abraham Lincoln.

Make Haste

See then that ye walk circumspectly, not as fools, but as wise. Redeeming the time, because the days are evil.

Ephesians 5:15–16

Let every flying hour confess
I gain the gospel fresh renown;
And when my life and labours cease,
May I possess the promised crown.

To Abraham Lincoln, time was a precious commodity. It was one of the few things that could be lost forever. The future of America was at risk, and time was always of the essence. "There is not a moment of time to be lost," he sternly told Union soldiers. Do you often let time go by without taking advantage of the opportunity to make a difference? Lincoln relaxed and rested, but he also never let a waste of time ruin his chances for success. He was punctual, and he didn't procrastinate. Time can be your best friend or your worst enemy. And there's no stopping it. If you try to make Lincoln's timely philosophy a part of your life and remember not to lose moments of time that you can't ever take back, you'll never regret your use of time.

Gather Intelligence, Then Decide

A good man sheweth favour, and lendeth: he will guide his affairs with discretion.

Psalm 112:5

Believers love what God commands,
And in his ways delight;
Their gracious words and holy hands
Show that their faith is right.

Their converse is with God above,
Their labours bless mankind;
Their works of mercy, peace and love,
Through Christ acceptance find.

Have you ever made a hasty decision, only to later regret it because you didn't fully consider the consequences? Lincoln lived by a simple rule: Get all the facts before you make a decision. He said, "It is proper that I should avail myself of all the information and all the time at my command in order that when the time arrives, I shall be able to take the ground which I deem the best and safest and from which I may have no occasion to swerve." Before you make your next decision, ask yourself if you have all the information. Make sure you consider the consequences of your actions first. Because after a decision is made, there's usually no turning back.

On Anxiety and Impatience

Let your moderation be known unto all men. The Lord is at hand.

Philippians 4:5

We'll look on all the toys below
With such disdain as angels do;
And wait the call that bids us rise
To mansions promised in the skies.

Can a person be too patient? Lincoln was patient, but he wasn't so patient as to be ineffective. He had the fortitude to wait, but he didn't wait so long as to miss opportunities. "While I am anxious, please do not suppose I am impatient," he once said. Being patient does not mean endurance without action. It does not mean you should be tolerant to the extent that people and situations get the best of you. It simply means to wait for the right time to take action. Lincoln was anxious to win the war, but he was also patient. But he didn't let his patience give his enemies time to take advantage, and he didn't let his anxiety allow his enemies the opportunity to take advantage of hasty decisions.

Be Consistent

Not forsaking the assembling of ourselves together, as the manner of some is; but exhorting one another: and so much the more, as ye see the day approaching.

Hebrews 10:25

Oh let me always find a place,
Within the temples of thy grace;
Till God command my last remove,
To dwell in temples made above!

As a political leader, Lincoln often found himself in situations where other people wanted him to change his views. Friends and colleagues would often beg him to alter a policy, change an opinion, or amend a belief. We all face similar pressures in life. People push us to modify our values and way of life. Lincoln always had an easy answer for those who wanted him to change. "No party can command respect which sustains this year what it opposed last," he said. For Lincoln, taking a stand was all about respect. He refused to run with whims and trends, but instead stood by what he had always believed. While the short-term consequences of his consistency might have seemed unpopular, the long-term results were what might have been expected. Everyone always knew where Abraham Lincoln stood. Can people say the same of you?

To Be Fair

Whatsoever things are true, whatsoever things are honest, whatsoever things are just, whatsoever things are pure, whatsoever things are lovely, whatsoever things are of good report; if there be any virtue, and if there be any praise, think on these things.

Philippians 4:8

Father of eternal grace,
Glorify thyself in me;
Meekly beaming in my face,
May the world thine image see.

One doesn't have to be very old to spot an injustice. Even children complain about things that are unfair. We all feel, at times, that our circumstances are unreasonable or excessive. We all feel like we're not treated equally or that we're the victims of bias. Some people are actually preoccupied with all the things in their lives that aren't fair. Lincoln was aware of man's obsession with the fairness principle. He once reminded his cabinet, "There is no keeping men silent when they feel they are wronged by their friends." By that Lincoln meant to treat other people fairly, with justice. You can't control whether others treat you fairly, but you can control how fairly you treat others.

Where to Find Bad Advice

I keep under my body, and bring it into subjection: lest that by any means, when I have preached to others, I myself should be a castaway.

1 Corinthians 9:27

> *When thy statutes I forsake,*
> *When my graces dimly shine,*
> *When my covenant I break,*
> *Jesus, then remember thine:*
> *Check my wanderings*
> *By look of love divine.*

It's surprising how people rely on advice from those they don't even know. Advice isn't very hard to find. Everyone, it seems, is glad to give you a piece of their mind. They'll tell you what to do and how to do it. No matter what the subject or the circumstance, everyone has an answer. That is why it is so important to be careful whose advice you take. Lincoln had a rule: "The interference of outsiders generally does more harm than good. It breeds confusion and, with it, delays and neglect." Lincoln recommended finding advice among one's friends, those who know you best and care for you the most. Otherwise, you'll get advice you can't trust.

Be Useful

And one of [the ten lepers] when he saw that he was healed, turned back, and with a loud voice glorified God.

Luke 17:15

What thanks I owe thee, and what love,
A boundless, endless store,
Shall echo through the realms above,
When time shall be no more.

When Abraham Lincoln evaluated another person's qualifications for a job, he ordinarily looked at only one thing. He called it "usefulness," or effectiveness. He wanted to know if the person was not only a hard worker, but a smart worker. Lincoln had no patience for people he called "idle" and even less for those who kept busy but didn't achieve much. "The habits of our whole species fall into three great classes—usefulness, labor, and idleness. Of these the first only is meritorious, and to it all the products of labor rightfully belong; but the two latter, while they exist, are heavy pensioners upon the first, robbing it of a large portion of its just rights," he wrote. Work on your usefulness. If you're idle, get busy. If you're busy, make sure you're busy working on the right things. Then you'll be the kind of person Lincoln would hire.

When You're Down and Out, Don't Tear Down Others

Whatsoever ye do in word or deed, do all in the name of the Lord Jesus, giving thanks to God and the Father by him.

Colossians 3:17

Whate'er I say or do,
Thy glory be my aim;
My offerings all be offered through
His ever blessed name.

When things aren't going your way, are you tempted to make sure things don't go well for others too? Do you spend precious time and energy complaining about your situation and tearing down other people? If so, that might be the very thing that's keeping you down. Lincoln said, "Let not him who is houseless pull down the house of another; but let him labor diligently and build one for himself, thus by example assuring that his own shall be safe from violence when built." Lincoln's advice is simple. Focus on your problem, not someone else's problem, and climb out of it. The more time you spend thinking about the other guy, the less time you have to figure out how to solve your own problems. If your house has been destroyed, build it up. Don't tear down your neighbor's house.

Be Diligent

In every thing give thanks: for this is the will of God in Christ Jesus concerning you.

1 Thessalonians 5:18

Praise to God, immortal praise,
For the love that crowns our days;
Bounteous Source of every joy,
Let thy praise our tongues employ.

"The leading rule for a lawyer, as for the man of every other calling, is diligence," wrote Abraham Lincoln. A person can be smart, strong, well-dressed, and even have integrity but still not achieve much in life. The key, according to Lincoln, is to be diligent. To Lincoln that meant to persevere and to be thorough and meticulous. It meant to make a plan and follow it and to be effective. But mostly it meant to follow through on your task and not give up. Lincoln knew that diligence could make up for lack in many other areas. He had little education, no money, and a life full of pain and grief. Those are not normally the makings of a successful person. But Lincoln was diligent. He made up his mind and stuck to his plan. Are you diligent? If you're disappointed in the things you're achieving in your life, maybe you just lack the diligence to make them happen. Decide today to be more diligent.

Read, Read, Read

Jesus said unto him, Verily I say unto thee, To day shalt thou be with me in paradise.

Luke 23:43

There is a land of pure delight,
Where saints immortal reign;
Infinite day excludes the night,
And pleasures banish pain.

There everlasting spring abides,
And never-withering flowers:
Death, like a narrow sea, divides
This heavenly land from ours.

Lincoln was a reader. He believed people could improve themselves simply by reading books. As a young child, the only book he had to read was the Bible. He read his Bible so much he once commented that he wished he had another book besides it! Later in life Lincoln read whatever he could get his hands on. Once a young man asked President Lincoln how he too could become a lawyer. The man had no money and little education. Lincoln replied, "If you wish to be a lawyer, attach no consequence to the *place* you are in or the *person* you are with; but get books, sit down anywhere and go reading for yourself. That will make a lawyer of you quicker than any other way." Likewise, you can become whatever you desire in life, if only you'll read.

Be Single-Minded

There shall in no wise enter into it any thing that defileth, neither whatsoever worketh abomination, or maketh a lie: but they which are written in the Lamb's book of life.

Revelation 21:27

The soul, from sin for ever free,
Shall mourn its power no more,
But clothed in spotless purity,
Redeeming love adore.

Abraham Lincoln believed the only way for an organization, be it a country or a company, to succeed was for one person to be at the helm. Organizations could not be run by committee, he surmised. "Some single mind must be master, else there will be no agreement in anything," he said. For Lincoln, this meant two things. First, it meant that to win the war, he must be a strong commander in chief. There would be no winning if he was weak. Second, it meant that the country itself must submit itself to a single mind, that mind being Providence. Lincoln believed God was to be at the helm of the nation and at the helm of each individual life. If not, there would be internal chaos and confusion. No country, no organization, and no person could stand without the governance of a single mind.

The Value of Work

Thou wilt show me the path of life: in thy presence is fulness of joy; at thy right hand there are pleasures for evermore.

Psalm 16:11

Love, in an ever-deepening tide,
O'er all the plains above
Spreads, like a sea immensely wide —
For God himself is Love.

Of all the values and principles Lincoln believed in, the idea that a person should work hard was probably the one he believed in most. Abraham Lincoln was a frontiersman, and frontiersmen worked hard just to survive. They built their own homes and plowed their own land. So as Lincoln matured and ultimately became president of the United States, his strong work ethic stuck with him. It was a part of his nature, and it amazed his colleagues who were raised in more abundant surroundings. "The mode is very simple," he told them, "though laborious and tedious . . . work, work, work is the main thing." Not all of us have learned Lincoln's work ethic. But by gleaning his words, we can learn to work, work, work too.

What Other People Say
(Doesn't Always Matter)

They serve him day and night in his temple: and he that sitteth on the throne shall dwell among them.

Revelation 7:15

And swift to do his high behest
Each spirit wings its flight;
And virtue glows on every breast,
A gem of purest light.

Abraham Lincoln was one of those people nobody expected to succeed. He was underrated. His appearance wasn't impressive. He was clumsy, awkward, and easy to poke fun at. "Nobody ever expected me to be president," he quipped shortly after being elected to the nation's highest office. But Lincoln learned what many people never do. It doesn't matter much what other people say or think. What matters is what you think about yourself, about your own diligence and will to succeed. Lincoln paid little attention to the views of others. He was self-taught and self-initiated. He learned to lean only on God, whom he could always trust, and to press on. And he learned to press on knowing that God would have his way.

Those Who Say Little, Say Much

He delivereth me from mine enemies: yea, thou liftest me above those that rise up against me.

Psalm 18:48

Foes are round us, but we stand
On the borders of our land:
Jesus, God's exalted Son,
Bids us undismay'd go on:
Onward then we gladly press
Through this earthly wilderness.

Do you tend to do the listening or the talking? If you were Abraham Lincoln, you'd spend most of your time listening, taking in everything, rather than spouting off. "I am rather inclined to silence," he said, "and whether that be wise or not, it is at least more unusual nowadays to find a man who can hold his tongue than to find one who cannot." The view Lincoln took was to gather as much information as possible, learn as much as possible, and then speak only words that were well thought out. Too many people, he believed, did the opposite. They listened and learned very little but talked a lot. Lincoln knew the secret to success was not talking your way there, but listening and learning your way there. And when Lincoln spoke, people listened. They trusted his words because he didn't expend them uselessly.

Admit Your Mistake

I give unto them eternal life; and they shall never perish, neither shall any man pluck them out of my hand.

John 10:28

"Unnumber'd years of bliss
I to my sheep will give;
And while my throne unshaken stands
Shall all my chosen live."

Enough, my gracious Lord,
Let faith triumphant cry;
My heart can on this promise live,
Can with this promise die.

Once when angrily confronted by a member of his cabinet about an erroneous statement Lincoln had made earlier, Lincoln was quick to confess his mistake. "I . . . wish to make the personal acknowledgment that you were right and I was wrong," he said calmly. Lincoln's honest and prompt reply silenced his colleague. Abraham Lincoln was always quick to make a confession. He knew most people weren't and that, by admitting his guilt, there was little more his agitator could say. Usually when one says, "I'm sorry," that's the end of the matter. Saying "I'm sorry" is probably one of the most disarming and beguiling ways to make up for a fault. Lincoln's use of confession helped him to maintain the respect of his peers, and it helped others to be more transparent and honest with him. If you admit your mistakes more often, you'll never have to worry about being wrong.

You Control Less Than You Think

In the time of trouble he shall hide me in his pavilion: in the secret of his tabernacle shall he hide me; he shall set me upon a rock.

Psalm 27:5

When I can trust my all with God,
In trial's fearful hour —
Bow, all resign'd, beneath his rod,
And bless his sparing power;
A joy springs up amid distress,
A fountain in the wilderness.

When things are going well, we like to think we have control over our lives. We think we can manage things without anyone's help. But when things turn bad, we wonder what happened. During the worst days of the Civil War, when everything seemed to turn against President Lincoln, he plainly admitted how very little control he had over events. "I claim not to have controlled events, but confess plainly that events have controlled me," he admitted. For Lincoln, the admission was probably a humbling experience. He had worked hard to inspire the Union and to command his troops, yet nothing went as planned. Do you feel as if nothing is going as you planned? The truth is, things rarely go as we thought they would. Like Lincoln, it's best to admit we can't control events. They control us. When you do this and then give events up to God, you'll have less stress.

Be Loyal

My grace is sufficient for thee: for my strength is made perfect in weakness.

2 Corinthians 12:9

Why should I fear the darkest hour,
Or tremble at the tempter's power!
Jesus vouchsafes to be my tower.

Though hot the fight, why quit the field?
Why must I either fear or yield,
Since Jesus is my mighty shield?

Have you promised the people closest to you that you'll never leave them? Do you plan to keep your promise? Unfortunately, there's a lot of deserting these days. Vows are broken, promises are breached. President Lincoln knew the only way to instill confidence in his fellow Americans was to vow he'd be there for them to the end. Making such a promise to always be there, no matter what the circumstances, is the best way to build confidence and trust. "Many free countries have lost their liberty, and *ours may* lose hers; but if she shall, be it my proudest plume, not that I was the *last* to desert, but that I *never* deserted her," Lincoln proclaimed. By saying, "I will not forsake you," Lincoln knew the country would trust him and his decision-making abilities. A vow is usually returned with the same. And by the Union's actions, it did indeed reciprocate on Lincoln's vow. Promise to be there, and you can count on support.

The Value of Repentance

Him that overcometh will I make a pillar in the temple of my God, and he shall go no more out.

Revelation 3:12

The everlasting doors
Shall soon the saints receive,
Above, with angel powers,
In glorious joy to live:
Far from a world of grief and sin,
With God eternally shut in.

We've all said things we wished we hadn't, especially in anger. When tempers flare, it's easy to hurt people by saying things we don't mean. Later, when the situation has calmed, the embarrassment of realizing what was said can often break a relationship. That's why it's always a good idea to hastily plead for forgiveness. Lincoln seldom lost his temper, but, when he did, he could say some pretty mean and nasty things. That's why he'd always follow up by begging for forgiveness. His friendships were more important than his pride, and he knew the sooner he tried to mend fences, the better. "It is always magnanimous to recant whatever we may have said in passion," advised Lincoln.

Admit It When You're Down

Because thou hast been my help, therefore in the shadow of
thy wings will I rejoice.

Psalm 63:7

Since thou hast been my help,
To thee my spirit flies;
And on thy watchful providence
My cheerful hope relies.

You'd think Abraham Lincoln never got depressed. A man
of so much moderation and calm needn't get disheartened. On
the contrary, however, Lincoln got pretty glum at times. He
wrote in his journal, "I am now the most miserable man living. If what I feel were equally distributed to the whole human
family, there would not be one cheerful face on the earth."
Now that sounds like a depressed man! Today doctors might
write him a prescription for making that statement. What
helped Lincoln was that he was honest with himself and others in his depression. He didn't hide it. And by writing about
it, he was able to get it off his chest. Of the many lessons we
can learn from Lincoln, this one may be the most unexpected.
When you get depressed, write about it. Admit it, and then
you'll be better able to climb out.

Be Teachable

Weeping may endure for a night, but joy cometh in the morning.

Psalm 30:5

When comforts are declining,
He grants the soul again,
A season of clear shining,
To cheer it after rain.

Abraham Lincoln was raised to work a farm, not to read books. Later in life he recalled his upbringing as a constant fight with trees, logs, and grubs. "There was absolutely nothing to excite ambition for education," he said. Young Abe Lincoln attended some schools, but for less than a year altogether. "Still, somehow," he remembered, "I could read, write, and cipher to the Rule of Three." How did he learn to read and write? He was teachable. Despite having no formal education, he learned what he could from his surroundings. His teacher was life itself, and he took every opportunity to learn from it. Later in life Lincoln took to the books. He studied the Bible and the classics, and he never missed an opportunity to read the daily news. Lincoln exemplifies the fact that any person can learn with or without a teacher. If you are teachable, you can teach yourself.

Haste Makes Waste

These things I have spoken unto you, that in me ye might have peace. In the world ye shall have tribulation: but be of good cheer; I have overcome the world.

John 16:33

The path of sorrow, and that path alone,
Leads to the land where sorrow is unknown.
No traveller e'er reached that bless'd abode,
Who found not thorns and briars in his road.

It's hard to make a mistake when you're careful. Think about some of the stupidest things you've ever done. Were you being cautious at the time? Or did you do the thing in haste? We all regret those times we simply could have slowed down a bit or taken a few extra moments to take a second look. That's how Lincoln looked at life too. "I frequently make mistakes myself, in the many things I am compelled to do hastily," he said. Lincoln was saying that when he did something in haste, he often did the wrong thing. It's a simple lesson—one we already know. But it's something Lincoln talked about a lot. He taught himself to be contemplative and pensive before acting. Slow down, think about it, and then make your next move. The moments you spend thinking will almost always be worth the time you might lose in making an error.

When to Toot Your Own Horn

Now no chastening for the present seemeth to be joyous, but grievous: nevertheless afterward it yieldeth the peaceable fruit of righteousness unto them which are exercised thereby.

Hebrews 12:11

Our hearts are fasten'd to this world
By strong and endless ties;
But every sorrow cuts a string,
And urges us to rise.

"Sound your own horn," said Lincoln, "for behold, if you sound not your own horn, your horn shall not be sounded." This lesson seems a bit odd. It sounds like Lincoln was telling his colleague to boast a little, to do a little self-promotion. And that's not like Lincoln. He was self-tempered, not prone much toward showing off. What Lincoln was really saying is this: If you're going to be heard, you have to speak. Nobody succeeds by keeping quiet. And nobody else is going to take up your cause and wave your flag. Abraham Lincoln was a quiet man. At the same time, he didn't waver from making himself heard. He'd get up in front of crowds, at train stations and on street corners, bellowing his case. If you feel like you're not getting anywhere, maybe you need to speak up. Toot your horn!

Be Grateful

In whom we have redemption through his blood, even the forgiveness of sins.

Colossians 1:14

O Lamb of God, thy precious blood
Shall never lose its power,
Till all the ransom'd church of God
Is saved, to sin no more.

E'er since, by faith, I saw the stream
Thy flowing wounds supply,
Redeeming love has been my theme,
And shall be till I die.

President Lincoln expressed great appreciation for things. At dinners, receptions, and banquets, he would often give lengthy mentions of his gratefulness. And he would follow up with notes and letters with generous compliments. At one such reception, Lincoln commented, "Most heartily do I thank you for this magnificent reception, and while I cannot take to myself any share of the compliment thus paid, more than that which pertains to a mere instrument—an accidental instrument, perhaps I should say—of a great cause, I yet must look upon it as a most magnificent reception and, as such, most heartily do I thank you for it." Now that's a grateful man! People appreciated Lincoln's humble approach to saying "thank you." Do you remember to say "thank you"? It's one of the easiest ways to win affection and build support.

Owe No Debts

Being justified freely by his grace through the redemption that is in Christ Jesus.

Romans 3:24

No righteousness but his we own,
No ransom but his blood alone:
While on the Father's name we call,
Our faith pleads Christ as all in all.

Lincoln didn't owe anything to anybody. He didn't believe in debt. Contrary to how modern culture views debt, Lincoln was morally opposed to it. "I never keep anybody's money which I collect an hour longer than I can find a chance to turn it over to him," he said. Lincoln's aversion to debt was a biblical principle he learned at a very young age and practiced throughout his life. His reasons were simple. He believed indebtedness meant a part of a person was owned by another. It constrained one's freedom and clouded one's judgment. It meant another person controlled a part of one's life. So Lincoln returned money fast. This lesson is one few people would heed today but one to which Lincoln held fast, as did most people of his time.

Acknowledge Evil

For if, when we were enemies, we were reconciled to God by the death of his Son, much more, being reconciled, we shall be saved by his life.

Romans 5:10

> *Let us love, and sing, and wonder;*
> *Let us praise the Saviour's name:*
> *He has hush'd the law's loud thunder,*
> *He has quench'd Mount Sinai's flame:*
> *He has wash'd us with his blood,*
> *He has brought us nigh to God.*

To Lincoln, the difference between good and evil was plain. It was plain because God made it plain. There was no gray, just black and white, good and bad. "God did not place good and evil before man, telling him to make his choice," wrote Lincoln. "On the contrary, he did tell him there was one tree, the fruit of which he should not eat upon pain of certain death." Sometimes people blur the lines between good and evil in the name of tolerance. Lincoln had little time for this kind of tolerance. He wouldn't tolerate lesser degrees of justice, half-freedoms, and unequal treatment of others. He simply believed in good and evil. He acknowledged that evil existed, and he fought against it. Would Lincoln's moral precepts be tolerated today?

Actions Are Based on Motives

As many as received him, to them gave he power to become the sons of God, even to them that believe on his name.

John 1:12

Let others boast their ancient line,
In long succession great;
In the proud list, let heroes shine
And monarchs swell their state:
Descended from the King of kings,
Each saint a nobler title sings.

When he was confronted with tough questions, Lincoln would sometimes respond with another question. "Why build a cage if you expect to catch no birds?" he once asked when confronted with the suspicious actions of an enemy. Lincoln's point was that if someone is up to "no good," look at the person's motives. Lincoln often tried to look at people at a deep level. He tried to look at their hearts and intentions before making judgments, because he believed actions were based on motives. If you're skeptical about another person, or if you're trying to decide if someone near you may have bad intentions, try looking at their motives. Are they building a cage? If so, why?

Be Careful When Taking a Compliment

Let us consider one another to provoke unto love and to good works.

Hebrews 10:24

> *Awake, my soul, awake, my love,*
> *And serve my Saviour here below,*
> *In works which all the saints above*
> *And holy angels cannot do.*

Sometimes you shouldn't heed too much advice from friends and family. It may be too biased. "I have a good deal of good news from New York; but, of course, it is from friends and is one-sided," Lincoln told his wife. So he took the news only half-heartedly, knowing that the truth might not be such good news. When you take a compliment from a friend, make sure you don't put too much weight on it. Look a little deeper and weigh all your options before going on the advice of those who like you. The news may not be so good when you find out what others are saying.

Respect Your Authorities

Now they desire a better country, that is, an heavenly: where-fore God is not ashamed to be called their God: for he hath prepared for them a city.

Hebrews 11:16

'Tis true, we are but strangers
And sojourners below;
And countless snares and dangers
Surround the path we go:
Though painful and distressing,
Yet there's a rest above,
And onward we are pressing
To reach that land of love.

It seems like simple advice: Obey the authorities. But all too often it's neglected. Lincoln knew it was sometimes against man's nature to obey. Sometimes rebellion rules the hearts of men. So he was always quick to remind his troops to respect their commanders. "When differences arise between officers of the Government, the ranking officer must be obeyed," he told soldiers in the field. It was a biblical portent, to obey and respect authorities, and it is advice we can take today. Give the authorities in your life, at work or at home, their proper respect. It will make your life simpler and lead to better decisions.

Promote Peace

Lord, now lettest thou thy servant depart in peace, according to thy word: for mine eyes have seen thy salvation.

Luke 2:29–30

When we have number'd all our years,
And stand, at length, on Jordan's brink;
Though the flesh fail with mortal fears,
Oh! let not then the spirit sink:
But strong in faith, and hope, and love,
Plunge through the stream to rise above.

It's not easy to be a peacemaker. It takes more than a sweet spirit and pleasant personality to bring people together. You've got to be tough-minded and resolute. Do you work hard to promote peace, or do you by bypass dissension? Abraham Lincoln knew how hard it was to be a peacemaker. "I shall do all that is in my power to promote peaceful settlement of our present difficulties," he said. But to make peace, he'd sometimes have to be unyielding in his beliefs and his approach. "There is none who would do more than to preserve it [peace]. But it may be necessary to put the foot down firmly," he added. When you see conflict and dissension around you, put your foot down and demand a peaceful resolution.

Respect Your Enemies

Well done, thou good and faithful servant: thou hast been faithful over a few things, I will make thee ruler over many things: enter thou into the joy of thy lord.

Matthew 25:21

Soldier of Christ, well done!
Praise be thy new employ;
And while eternal ages run,
Rest in thy Saviour's joy.

Abraham Lincoln was always careful to respect both his friends and his enemies. He never treated people with disdain or disregard. He gave specific directions to his generals prior to their meeting with the Southern leader, Jefferson Davis: "You will proceed forthwith, and obtain, a conference for peace with the honorable Jefferson Davis, or any person by him authorized for that purpose. You will address him in entirely respectful terms, at all events, and in any that may be indispensable to secure the conference." By this time, the Union soldiers had developed a deep-seated hatred for the rebels—their enemy. Lincoln knew they might treat Davis poorly. But Lincoln demanded they treat Davis with respect. Do you respect others, even the ones you don't like? Not until you respect them can you expect like treatment.

On Quitting When You're Ahead

So when this corruptible shall have put on incorruption, and this mortal shall have put on immortality, then shall be brought to pass the saying that is written, Death is swallowed up in victory.

1 Corinthians 15:54

Where then thy triumph, Grave? and where thy sting,
O sullen Death? What terror dost thou bring?
We burst thine iron band, and soar on high—
Glory to Christ the Lord, who brings us victory!

Stick to it! Lincoln always encouraged his friends to stay the course and not give up. Sometimes when things start going against us, we're tempted to quit and start over at something else. One of Lincoln's friends once asked for advice when he was thinking about leaving his career in the military. "As you ask my advice, it is that if you are doing well, you had better stick to it. If you have a good start there and should give it up, you might not get it again, here or elsewhere." Lincoln's advice to finish what you start is timeless. It was true then and it's true for us today. You may never have another opportunity to start again, so stick with the task and finish it.

Remember Your Purpose

The Lamb which is in the midst of the throne shall feed them, and shall lead them unto living fountains of waters.

Revelation 7:17

The Lamb that fills the middle throne
Shall shed around his milder beams,
There shall they feast on his rich love,
And drink full joys from heavenly streams.

Change can be difficult. When you find yourself in a new job or career, a new place, or a new relationship, you might be tempted to go back. Once when a young cadet was tempted to leave a military academy, Lincoln gave him some advice that we can all heed today. "Your good mother tells me you are feeling very badly in your new situation. Allow me to assure you it is a perfect certainty that you will very soon feel better—quite happy—if you only stick to the resolution you have taken to procure a military education. I am older than you, have felt badly myself, and *know* what I tell you is true. Adhere to your purpose, and you will soon feel as well as you ever did. On the contrary, if you falter and give up, you will lose the power of keeping any resolution and will regret it all your life. Take the advice of a friend who, though he never saw you, deeply sympathizes with you, and stick to your purpose."

On the Art of Persuasion

He will dwell with them, and they shall be his people, and God himself shall be with them, and be their God.

Revelation 21:3

Oh glorious hour! Oh bless'd abode!
I shall be near and like my God;
And flesh and sin no more control
The sacred pleasures of the soul.

What's the best way to convince someone else to do something? Is it through fear, intimidation, and manipulation? Abraham Lincoln was a master at getting people to do what he wanted them to do. But he didn't use exploitive techniques to get his way. He used kindness and gentle persuasion. "When the conduct of men is designed to be influenced, *persuasion,* kind, unassuming persuasion, should ever be adopted." Instead of using the power of the presidency, Lincoln was known to sit down with his opponents and engage them in long conversation. He would ask questions and with gentleness confront them with the truth. The result was usually to his benefit. He was able to persuade and influence without demeaning. The next time you need to get someone on your side, use the gentle art of persuasion, not fear or intimidation. You'll be surprised at the results.

On Planning

God shall wipe away all tears from their eyes; and there shall be no more death, neither sorrow, nor crying, neither shall there be any more pain: for the former things are passed away.

Revelation 21:4

Joy and gladness banish sighs,
Perfect love dispels their fears,
And for ever from their eyes,
God shall wipe away all tears.

Do you want to learn how to make better decisions? Too often we make decisions in a vacuum. Blinded by our past and surroundings, we take off in one direction without knowing where we stand. Lincoln's decision-making strategy was simple. "If we could first know *where* we are and *whither* we are tending, we could then better judge *what* to do and *how* to do it," he explained. Before making any decision in your life, big or small, it's vital to know where you stand. It's important to look at your past and understand the present before you make any decisions that affect your future. If you're fuzzy as to how you ended up in such a mess, maybe you should do some reflecting before taking action. Otherwise, you might make the same mistake twice. If you know where you are and how you got there, you can better judge what to do.

Be Forthright with Your Enemies

They which shall be accounted worthy to obtain that world, and the resurrection from the dead, neither marry nor are given in marriage: neither can they die any more: for they are equal unto the angels.

Luke 20:35–36

There pain and sickness never come,
And grief no more complains;
Health triumphs in immortal bloom,
And endless pleasure reigns.

How do children get their way with their parents? They demand explanations. They want to know why or why not. And every parent knows that such conversations can't be won. The child will bicker and wrangle, trying his or her best to win over the parent. Instead, the parent will say simply, "Because that's the way it is." End of story. Abraham Lincoln believed the same strategy worked with adults. "I wish no explanation made to our enemies," he said. "What they want is a squabble and a fuss; and that they can have if we explain, and they cannot have if we don't." That's why Lincoln refused to sit down with the Confederacy in search of a compromise. He knew that would have been futile. If you want to win an argument, sometimes the best strategy is to say nothing at all.

Willpower

I know that my redeemer liveth, and that he shall stand at the latter day upon the earth: and though after my skin worms destroy this body, yet in my flesh shall I see God.

Job 19:25–26

Though worms may waste this with'ring clay,
When flesh and spirit sever;
My soul shall see eternal day,
And dwell with God for ever.

Do you sometimes wish you had more education? Maybe if you had learned a little more, graduated, or gone after that next degree, you could have achieved more in life. Abraham Lincoln was proof that a good education costs nothing. He was evidence that one doesn't have to be wealthy to learn. He had very little in terms of money and resources, even as an adult. But he took every opportunity to teach himself, through books, newspapers, and mostly, through experience. He was self-educated. Isn't all learning ultimately self-education? We all know people who've attended the "best" schools but never learned much. And then there's the successful small businessman who never finished high school but learned a trade and made the best of himself. "In this country one can scarcely be so poor but that, if he *will*, he *can* acquire sufficient education to get through the world respectably," wrote Lincoln. If you want the best education, it's never too late, and you can get started today. It takes time, not money.

Pray Harder

Beloved, now are we the sons of God, and it doth not yet appear what we shall be: but we know that, when he shall appear, we shall be like him; for we shall see him as he is.

1 John 3:2

Him eye to eye we there shall see,
Our face like his shall shine:
Oh, what a glorious company,
When saints and angels join!

President Lincoln would sometimes interview Union soldiers who had been held captive by the Confederacy but had escaped. Often these freed soldiers could give valuable information about rebel troop movements or new uses of weaponry. Once Lincoln learned that Confederate troops were often seen praying with each other. This was quite discouraging to the president. "The rebel soldiers are praying with a good deal more earnestness than our own troops," he complained, "and expecting God to favor their side." Prayer was important to Abraham Lincoln, and when his side was being "out-prayed," he was let down. Might God listen more to those who prayed harder? It certainly seems likely that God would answer those who asked before those who didn't. What about you? Are you being "out-prayed"?

Stand Watch

We know that if our earthly house of this tabernacle were dissolved, we have a building of God, an house not made with hands, eternal in the heavens.

2 Corinthians 5:1

There is a home for weary souls,
By sin and sorrow driven;
When toss'd on life's tempestuous shoals,
Where storms arise, and ocean rolls,
'Tis found above—in heaven.

President Lincoln worked hard to secure freedom and justice for America. He spent many a late night poring over plans, tactics, and strategies. He traveled to the front lines, spent time with his generals, and wrote thousands of letters to garner support for the war effort. No man had worked harder. Yet the war dragged on. At times it seemed nothing was going right, that all might be lost. And when disgruntled friends and colleagues began to give in, Lincoln's morale weakened. But instead of giving in, Lincoln did what he always did in times of trouble—he stood firm. Lincoln once told a friend, "The most we can do now is to watch events and be as well prepared as possible for any turn things may take." He didn't quit. He continued to prepare, and he watched for things to turn his way. You can do the same as Lincoln. When you're at your wits' end, just keep on going, and watch for an opportunity.

Inspire Confidence

Now we see through a glass, darkly; but then face to face: now I know in part; but then shall I know even as also I am known.

1 Corinthians 13:12

As through a glass I dimly see
The wonders of thy love;
How little do I know of thee,
Or of the joys above!

'Tis but in part I know thy will —
I bless thee for the sight —
When will thy love the rest reveal
In glory's clearer light?

What's the best way to inspire confidence? How do you get others to follow you? In order to lead the Union to victory during the Civil War, Abraham Lincoln had to inspire the confidence of the people. If they wouldn't follow his lead, he couldn't show the way. So he traveled through the Union asking for support. Often when he'd meet with crowds of citizens, he'd point to the American flag, sometimes holding it in his hands. "Standing as I do, with my hand upon this staff, and under the folds of the American flag, I ask you to stand by me as long as I stand by it," he'd implore. Crowds would cheer and applaud and leave the meeting inspired. What did Lincoln do to inspire confidence? He gave the people a cause—freedom, justice, and liberty. If you want to inspire those around you, do the same—give them a cause.

Don't Fear Failure

Henceforth there is laid up for me a crown of righteousness, which the Lord, the righteous judge, shall give me at that day.

2 Timothy 4:8

God has laid up in heaven for me
A crown which cannot fade;
The righteous Judge, in that great day,
Shall place it on my head.

During the fall of 1864, it looked like the Union might lose the war. Robert E. Lee and his troops had made their way into Pennsylvania. Despite the Union having more men and resources, the Confederacy was winning. During these desperate days, the morale among Union troops and citizens began to falter. Lincoln's duty was to stir spirits as much as anything. Have you ever found yourself in a situation where things looked bleak and everyone else around you was giving up? What did you do about it? Listen to what Lincoln said: "The *probability* that we may fall in the struggle *ought not* to deter us from the support of a cause we believe to be just."

Morality Unites

Whilst we are at home in the body, we are absent from the Lord: . . . we are confident, I say, and willing rather to be absent from the body, and to be present with the Lord.

2 Corinthians 5:6, 8

In that bright city I would dwell,
With that bless'd church the Saviour praise,
And, safe, redeem'd from death and hell,
Sit at his feet through endless days.

"Moral principle is all, or nearly all, that unites us of the North," proclaimed Lincoln to an exasperated Union. Sometimes it's difficult to stay united in times of trouble. The daily trials and tribulations of life can soften our resolve and cause us to give up. This is true for families, businesses, churches, and even nations. When times get really tough, remember Lincoln's advice. Remember that principles and values should keep you going. Look to them and not to your troubles. During the Civil War, moral principle was sometimes all that was left to hang on to. When the Union was tempted to give up, Lincoln reminded them why they were fighting—for freedom and equality.

On Core Beliefs

There remaineth a rest to the people of God.

Hebrews 4:9

> *Oh where shall rest be found,*
> *Rest for the weary soul?*
> *'Twere vain the ocean-depths to sound,*
> *Or pierce to either pole.*
>
> *Beyond this vale of tears,*
> *There is a life above,*
> *Unmeasured by the flight of years —*
> *And all that life is love.*

There are some things in life worth fighting for. But all too often people end up fighting for things that aren't important. How many relationships have been ruined over temporal things like money or power? Abraham Lincoln once said, "We have to fight this battle [the Civil War] on principle, and upon principle alone." Lincoln knew how important it was to look only to his core beliefs, his beliefs in equality and liberty, when he made important decisions during the war. Are you basing your decisions on your core beliefs, or are you fighting for things that won't matter later on in life? Try to base your life on the things that are most important to you—your values and morals. Look to those things when you are making decisions, and later on in life you won't regret the paths you chose.

Principles Aren't Elastic

Not by works of righteousness which we have done, but according to his mercy he saved us, by the washing of regeneration, and renewing of the Holy Ghost.

Titus 3:5

Vain is every outward rite,
Unless thy grace be given:
Nothing but thy life and light,
Can form a soul for heaven.

Do you sometimes bend your morals, giving in to temptations just a little bit? We're all tempted from time to time to give up the things we believe in for some temporal pleasure. Sometimes we forget our core values and let temptation get the best of us. Abraham Lincoln once reminded a friend, "Important principles may, and must be, inflexible." Don't let your values be elastic. Don't stretch them too far, allowing yourself to disavow the things that are most important to you. When you stretch or bend your principles, you may end up broken. Lincoln knew the importance of being rigid and firm when it came to important principles. He didn't give in and fought hard for what he believed in. What if Lincoln had given in? What if he let up and freed only half the slaves? Don't let temptation get the best of you—be inflexible.

Be Relentless

Whereby are given unto us exceeding great and precious promises: that by these ye might be partakers of the divine nature, having escaped the corruption that is in the world through lust.

2 Peter 1:4

Blessed are the sons of God;
They are brought with Christ's own blood;
They produce the fruits of grace
In the works of righteousness:
Born of God, they hate all sin;
God's pure word remains within.

Judge Lyle Dickey told a story about Abraham Lincoln's persistence. When the Kansas-Nebraska Anti-Slavery Bill was announced, he was with Lincoln attending court. One day several persons, including himself and Lincoln, were discussing the slavery question. Judge Dickey contended that slavery was an institution the Constitution recognized. Lincoln argued that ultimately slavery must become extinct. "After a while," said Judge Dickey, "everyone went to bed." I remember that Lincoln sat up in his night shirt on the edge of the bed arguing the point with me. Early in the morning I woke up, and there was Lincoln half sitting up in bed. "Dickey," said he, "I tell you this nation cannot exist half slave and half free." Lincoln just wouldn't give up. It's that kind of relentless persistence that helped Lincoln win the White House.

On Kindness

By him all that believe are justified from all things, from which ye could not be justified by the law of Moses.

Acts 13:39

Jesus, thy blood and righteousness
My beauty are, and glorious dress;
'Midst flaming worlds, in these array'd,
With joy shall I lift up my head.

"My first impression of Abe Lincoln was made by one of his kind deeds," said a lady in Springfield, Illinois. Her story teaches a simple lesson about kindness. She was going on her first railroad trip but failed to call for her trunk. "I realized, in a panic of grief, that I would miss the train," she said. "I was standing by the gate, my hat and gloves on, sobbing as if my heart would break, when Mr. Lincoln came by. He asked me, 'What's the matter?' at which time I explained my dilemma. Before I knew what he was going to do, he had shouldered the trunk and was striding out of the yard. Down the street he went, fast as his long legs could carry him, I trotting behind, drying my tears as I went. We reached the station in time. Mr. Lincoln put me on the train, kissed me good-bye, and told me to have a good time." Lincoln didn't seek to impress with intellect or prowess but with kindness. His simple acts of kindness impressed upon others that his heart and motives were pure. The next time you seek to impress, try an act of kindness.

On Fair Trades

I am the vine, ye are the branches: He that abideth in me, and I in him, the same bringeth forth much fruit: for without me ye can do nothing.

John 15:5

Lord of the vineyard, we adore
That power and grace divine,
Which plants our wild, our barren souls,
In Christ the living Vine.

For ever there may I abide,
And from that vital root,
Be influence spread through every branch,
To form and feed the fruit.

When Lincoln was a young lawyer in Illinois, a certain judge asked him to trade horses. Lincoln knew the judge had a poor reputation for trades, so he planned to get the best of him. He wasn't going to be embarrassed or humiliated. He agreed to the trade, and at the appointed time the judge walked up leading the sorriest-looking specimen of a horse Lincoln had ever seen. A few moments later, Lincoln was seen approaching the judge with a wooden sawhorse on his shoulders. The laughter in the crowd only heightened when Lincoln set down his wooden horse and said, "Well, Judge, this is the first time I ever got the worst of it in a horse trade." Lincoln's jest proved a point. If you're going to offer a trade, make it fair. If you think you may get the best of another, you may have another thing coming.

See Past Your Problems

If children, then heirs; heirs of God, and joint-heirs with Christ.

Romans 8:17

> *Pronounce me, gracious God, thy son;*
> *Own me an heir divine;*
> *I'll pity princes on the throne,*
> *When I can call thee mine:*
> *Sceptres and crowns unenvied rise,*
> *And lose their lustre in mine eyes.*

"I suppose you found it necessary to make large concessions to Governor Blank as he returned from you perfectly satisfied," said an angry cabinet member. "Oh, no," President Lincoln replied, "I did not concede anything to the governor. Have you heard how that Illinois farmer got rid of a big log that was too big to haul out, too knotty to split, and too wet and soggy to burn? He ploughed around it," said Lincoln. "Now don't tell anybody, but that's the way I got rid of Governor Blank. I ploughed all round him, but it took me three hours to do it, and I was afraid every minute he'd see what I was up to." Lincoln never let a problem stop him. If he couldn't find a way through it, he found a way around it. Do you let problems stop you? Try Lincoln's approach before giving up. See past your problems and find a way around them.

Principle, Not Spectacle

For in him dwelleth all the fulness of the Godhead bodily. And ye are complete in him.

Colossians 2:9–10

Thy saints on earth, and those above,
Here join in sweet accord:
One body all in mutual love,
And thou their common Lord.
Yes, thou that body wilt present
Before thy Father's face,
Nor shall a wrinkle or a spot
Its beauteous form disgrace.

The day following the adjournment of the Baltimore Convention, at which President Lincoln was renominated for president, various people called to pay their respects. Being a humble man, Lincoln generally didn't like such things. While one delegation was being presented, the chairman said, "Mr. President, this is a most active and earnest friend of yours and the cause. He has, among other things, been good enough to paint a most beautiful portrait of yourself." President Lincoln took the gentleman's hand, and shaking it cordially, said with a merry voice, "I presume, sir, in painting your beautiful portrait, you took your idea of me from my principles and not from my person." Abraham Lincoln's humorous and humble reply also made a point. Lincoln ran on principle, not spectacle. He stood for values, not personal aggrandizement. No portrait could accurately illustrate who Lincoln was and why he ran for president. The whole idea of a portrait was, to Lincoln, preposterous. It wasn't about him. It was about his values.

Giving Responsibility

If any man sin, we have an advocate with the Father, Jesus Christ the righteous.

1 John 2:1

Look up, my soul, with cheerful eye,
  See where the great Redeemer stands —
Thy glorious Advocate on high,
  With precious incense in his hands.

He sweetens every humble groan,
  He recommends each broken prayer;
Recline thy hope on him alone,
  Whose power and love forbid despair.

One contributing factor to Lincoln's success was his handling of subordinates. When they did a good job, he was always generous with compliments. He praised and rewarded them. He also looked for opportunities to give more responsibility. When General Sherman captured Savannah in 1864, Lincoln wrote to him, "Now, the undertaking being a success, the honor is all yours; for I believe none of us went farther than to acquiesce. . . . But what next? I suppose it will be safer if I leave General Grant and yourself to decide." After paying tribute to Sherman, Lincoln gave him more freedom to make future decisions. Lincoln teaches us here to give credit where credit is due, and also to grant responsibility to those who deserve it. Sherman went on to achieve other victories as Lincoln continued to give him more leeway. Do you give compliments and responsibility?

Taking Responsibility

Paul, an apostle of Jesus Christ by the commandment of God
our Saviour, and Lord Jesus Christ, which is our hope.

1 Timothy 1:1

> *Jesus, my Lord, I look to thee;*
> *Where else can helpless sinners go?*
> *Thy boundless love shall set me free*
> *From all my wretchedness and woe.*

Shortly after the Union's loss of the second battle at Bull
Run, Lincoln's cabinet complained that it was General
McClellan's fault. They blamed him for not supporting field
commander John Pope during the battle with enough men
and resources, and they conjectured that McClellan abandoned Pope on purpose. Secretary of War Stanton was so furi-
ous that he demanded McClellan be dismissed. Lincoln
responded coolly, "No, Mr. Secretary, the order was mine; and
I will be responsible for it to the country." This act illustrated
the importance of taking responsibility when warranted. Lincoln had indeed made such an order, and he refused to let
another man bear the burden. Lincoln's decision to take
responsibility helped to build the confidence of his cabinet
and generals. They could trust that Lincoln wouldn't "bail
out" on them, that he would be honest and deal with integrity.
It caused them to do the same.

Be Flexible

When Christ, who is our life, shall appear, then shall ye also appear with him in glory.

Colossians 3:4

If my immortal Saviour lives,
Then my eternal life is sure;
His word a firm foundation gives,
Here let me build, and rest secure.

Here, O my soul, thy trust repose;
If Jesus is for ever mine,
Not death itself, that last of foes,
Shall break a union so divine.

Abraham Lincoln was a model of consistency. He always held fast to his views. One almost always knew where he or she stood with Lincoln. At the same time, Lincoln wasn't so stubborn that he wouldn't change his mind. He'd readily admit a mistake and alter a policy while still standing on firm ground. He also was on the lookout for better ways to do things. He said, "I shall do less whenever I shall believe what I am doing hurts the cause, and I shall do more whenever I shall believe doing more will help the cause. I shall try to correct errors when shown to be errors; and I shall adopt new views so fast as they appear to be true views," he once wrote to Horace Greeley. Have you made up your mind, or are you willing to be flexible? While certain values and principles don't change, plans and strategies may. Be like Lincoln and be prepared to invite change.

Healing a Wound

Now in Christ Jesus ye who sometime were far off are made nigh by the blood of Christ. For he is our peace.

Ephesians 2:13–14

"He is our peace"—for by his blood
Sinners are reconcil'd to God;
Sweet harmony is now restor'd,
And man beloved, and God ador'd.

Some in the Union were eager to take vengeance on the South after the war ended. Lincoln, who was not a vengeful person, was concerned. The purpose of the war was to unite, not divide, the country under freedom and justice. So when Union troops held a rally in front of the White House, Lincoln offered a dramatic gesture of benevolence. Lincoln ordered the playing of "Dixie." "I have always thought 'Dixie' one of the best tunes I have ever heard," he said. Lincoln knew it might be controversial to play the song and even presented the idea to the attorney general before making the decree. The idea was to let the nation know it was not time to take revenge. He knew the vast majority of the nation was ready to heal and would follow his lead. Are you a vengeful person? Or do you seek ways to unify and heal?

Say What You Mean

This is his name whereby he shall be called, The LORD our righteousness.

Jeremiah 23:6

Saviour divine, we know thy name,
And in that name we trust;
Thou art the Lord our righteousness,
Thou art thine Israel's boast.

That spotless robe which thou hast wrought,
Shall clothe us all around,
Nor by the piercing eye of God
One blemish shall be found.

"If there ever could be a proper time for mere catch arguments, that time surely is not now. In times like the present, men should utter nothing for which they would not willingly be responsible through time and eternity." Abraham Lincoln said what he meant and meant what he said. He knew the power of words. He took his words seriously, and people listened when he spoke. Do people listen to you? If not, maybe it's because you sometimes speak before you should. Remember, when you say something, it's hard to take it back. Say what you mean.

Share Your Sorrows

Know ye not that your body is the temple of the Holy Ghost which is in you, which ye have of God. . . ?

1 Corinthians 6:19

Creator Spirit! by whose aid
The world's foundations first were laid,
Come, visit every humble mind;
Come, pour thy joys on human kind:
From sin and sorrow set us free,
And make us temples worthy thee.

For those who were grieving, Abraham Lincoln was a good person to commiserate with. He was no stranger to loss, and he understood the healing power of sharing a sorrow with someone else. There was certainly lots of grief during and after the Civil War, for nearly everyone in the nation had lost loved ones. "I do not feel my own sorrows much more keenly than I do yours, when I know of them," wrote Lincoln to a grieving widow. Indeed, sharing your grief and sorrow with someone else helps. It helped Lincoln, and it can help you. Growing up on the frontier in the nineteenth century brought with it much loss. Lincoln lost his mother at the age of eight, a fiancée at the age of twenty, and other friends and family members. So when someone shared his or her grief with President Lincoln, he could sympathize.

Sorrow Brings Maturity

God hath from the beginning chosen you to salvation through sanctification of the Spirit and belief of the truth.

2 Thessalonians 2:13

Come, Holy Spirit, love divine,
Thy cleansing power impart;
Each erring thought and wish refine
That wanders near my heart.

Perhaps because Abraham Lincoln experienced so much grief throughout his life, especially in his younger years, he quickly developed maturity beyond his years. "In this sad world of ours, sorrow comes to all; and, to the young it comes with bitterest agony because it takes them unawares," Lincoln confided to a friend. "The older have learned to ever expect it." Although grief can be an agonizing experience, it can also teach us to have more compassion and sympathy. It helps us to see the finiteness of life. Lincoln learned all these things and expressed them in many ways as an adult. Although he most assuredly would have preferred not to have experienced so much loss, it's hard to say if he could have been such a great leader if he had not.

Be Resolute

That he would grant you, according to the riches of his glory,
to be strengthened with might by his Spirit in the inner man.

Ephesians 3:16

Assisted by his grace,
We still pursue our way;
And hope at last to reach the prize,
Secure in endless day.

What's the key to success? For Abraham Lincoln, the key to success wasn't what most might think. It wasn't brawn or brain power. Wealth was of least importance, and social skills didn't help much either. The key to success was simply the willingness to press on. It was the ability to look past one's circumstances, no matter how difficult, and to continue. "Always bear in mind that your own resolution to succeed is more important than any other one thing," he said to a friend. Lincoln was tenacious about his future. He was ambitious beyond all proportions and believed he could achieve most anything, albeit for the hand of Providence. By the time he was president, Lincoln was world-renowned for his ambition. His opponents knew he was a tough man to stop. Learn a lesson from Lincoln: Don't quit.

Watch Out for Disloyalties

Ye have not received the spirit of bondage again to fear; but ye have received the Spirit of adoption, whereby we cry, Abba, Father.

Romans 8:15

Assure my conscience of her part
In the Redeemer's blood,
And bear thy witness in my heart
That I am born of God.

President Lincoln once used the Bible to give a lesson on loyalty and devotion. He was concerned he might ultimately be betrayed, possibly by a good friend. When a colleague dismissed Lincoln's concerns, Lincoln reminded him, "The Savior of the world chose twelve disciples, and even one of that small number, selected by superhuman wisdom, turned out a traitor and a devil." Lincoln knew anyone could succumb to the power of sin. If Judas, a friend and eyewitness to the Son of God, could give him up for silver, certainly Lincoln too was at risk. Be careful not to trust too much. Know that disloyalty and a lack of devotion could be the very things that cause your demise.

Don't Give Dishonesty a Chance

Grieve not the holy Spirit of God, whereby ye are sealed unto the day of redemption.

Ephesians 4:30

Forbid it, Lord, that we
Who from thy hands receive
The Spirit's power to make us free,
Should e'er that Spirit grieve.

O keep our faith alive,
Help us to watch and pray;
Lest, by our carelessness, we drive
The sacred Guest away.

What's the best way to find the truth of a matter? Lincoln simply demanded it. He never gave his adversaries a chance to skirmish around the issue. He was pointed, frank, and forthright. Once when confronted with a possible lie, Lincoln told the man squarely, "You are compelled to speak; and your only alternative is to tell the *truth* or tell a *lie.* I cannot doubt which you would do." The man acquiesced and told the truth. If you make it plain that you won't stand for anything but the truth, everyone around you will acquiesce too. For those who stand for truth and righteousness, you cannot doubt what others will do.

Plant Yourself in the Truth

When he, the Spirit of truth, is come, he will guide you into all truth: for he shall not speak of himself; but whatsoever he shall hear, that shall he speak: and he will shew you things to come.

John 16:13

Thine inward teaching make me know
The mysteries of redeeming love,
The emptiness of things below,
And excellence of things above.

Is your life planted on solid ground? Do you know what you stand for and why? Understanding what you believe and why you believe it is vital to achieving success in life. If you're not sure what you believe, you're destined to become a follower rather than a leader. You can't lead if you don't know where you're going. And you can't know where you're going if you have no idea where you've been or where you are. Abraham Lincoln was a principled man. "I planted myself upon the truth and the truth only, so far as I knew it or could be brought to know it," he wrote. His views on freedom, justice, and liberty were rooted deep in the origins of the United States, in the Constitution, and in the Bible. Because he was so sure of himself, all of those who weren't so sure were glad to follow.

Go to God with Your Big Problems

Now therefore ye are no more strangers and foreigners, but fellow-citizens with the saints, and of the household of God.

Ephesians 2:19

The kindred links of life are bright,
Yet not so bright as those
In which Christ's favoured friends unite,
And each on each repose:
Where all the hearts in union cling,
With Him, the center and the spring.

The citizens of America elected Abraham Lincoln because they thought that he, in all of his wisdom, might find a way to avoid civil war. They believed he might unite the country and resolve the differences between North and South. Lincoln, however, knew this problem was too big for one man. If ever there was a big problem, it was what to do with a country divided. It involved friend against friend, brother against brother. Where did Lincoln go with his big problem? "Our problem now is can we, as a nation, continue together permanently and forever, half-slave and half-free? The problem is too mighty for me," he admitted. "May God in his mercy superintend a solution!" If you've been chosen to solve a big problem, you can go to the same place Lincoln went—to the Lord. God in his mercy can provide you with the strength and wisdom to find a solution.

The Bible Applies to Your Life

There is therefore now no condemnation to them which are in Christ Jesus, who walk not after the flesh, but after the Spirit.

Romans 8:1

> *O Love, thou bottomless abyss!*
> *My sins are swallow'd up in thee;*
> *Cover'd is my unrighteousness,*
> *From condemnation now I'm free;*
> *While Jesus' blood through earth and skies,*
> *"Mercy, free boundless mercy!" cries.*

Even in nineteenth-century America, people were doubting the Bible's relevance to their lives. Today the Bible is hardly mentioned as the standard for one's life or for a community or a nation. Abraham Lincoln, however, believed that the Bible was God's standard for all of life. He started reading the Bible at a young age and memorized much of its text. "The good old maxims of the Bible are applicable, and truly applicable, to human affairs," he proclaimed in a debate against Stephen Douglas. Lincoln leaned heavily on the Bible for both his personal and professional life. By following the principles in the Bible, he formed his views on freedom, justice, and equality. That is also how he persevered through some very tough times. The Bible was practical in 1865, and it still is today. If Lincoln could live by the Word of God, how much more can we today.

Faith in God Is Essential

Forasmuch then as the children are partakers of flesh and blood, he also himself likewise took part of the same; that through death he might destroy him that had the power of death, that is, the devil.

Hebrews 2:14

Dry up your tears, ye saints, and tell
How high your great Deliverer reigns;
Sing, how he spoiled the host of hell,
And led the tyrant Death in chains.

Where is your faith? Everyone has a measure of faith. You have to have faith in something, even to just get up in the morning and go out the front door. Some people put all their trust in themselves. Others rely on a loved one or a friend. Still others place their confidence in institutions. Abraham Lincoln placed his faith in God. "Faith in God is indispensable to successful statesmanship," he insisted. Why was faith in God important to Lincoln? Perhaps for two reasons Lincoln stood steadfast in his faith in God. First, he was desperate. The hugeness of his task humbled him to the point he had no choice but to turn to God. Second, his knowledge of Scripture surely caused him to turn to God when he needed the faith to endure. If you need faith to achieve, try putting your trust where Lincoln put his. Believe in God.

God's Word Gives Wisdom

Let Israel hope in the LORD: for with the LORD there is mercy, and with him is plenteous redemption. And he shall redeem Israel from all his iniquities.

Psalm 130:7–8

Fix'd on this ground will I remain,
Though my heart fail, and flesh decay;
This anchor shall my soul sustain,
When earth's foundations melt away:
Mercy's full power I then shall prove,
Lov'd with an everlasting love.

Abraham Lincoln leaned heavily on the Bible throughout his life and referred to it often. He used it in private and public meetings. He included passages from it in letters, and he used it to help develop some of his most memorable addresses. Lincoln once gave the reason why he relied on God's Word. "In regard to this great book, I have but to say, it is the best gift God has given to men. All the good Savior gave to the world was communicated through this book. But for it we could not know right from wrong. All things most desirable for man's welfare, here and hereafter, are to be found portrayed in it." Lincoln believed the Bible was the basis for the knowledge of good and evil, for faith to endure, and for the answers to life's most perplexing problems. If the greatest leader in American history believed this about the Bible, what do you believe?

God Never Forsakes

Which in time past were not a people, but are now the people of God: which had not obtained mercy, but now have obtained mercy.

1 Peter 2:10

Fill'd with holy emulation
Let us vie with those above:
Sweet the theme — a free salvation,
Fruit of everlasting love.

God never deserts. That's what the Bible says and what Abraham Lincoln believed. It's almost hard to imagine how a man who endured so much pain, grief, and sorrow could maintain so much faith in God. But Lincoln stood firm in his belief that God could be trusted, through loss, war, and even up to his death. Shortly before his assassination, Lincoln told a crowd of citizens, "I turn, then, and look to the great American people, and to that God who has never forsaken them." Have trials and tribulations reduced your faith in a God who never forsakes? Despite a seeming lack of evidence, Lincoln continued to believe. In fact, there were many times in his life when Lincoln was utterly disappointed, depressed, and dejected. There were times when God didn't seem to answer his prayers. But his knowledge that God really was with him carried him through. God never forsakes.

God Gives Safety

Who are kept by the power of God through faith unto salvation ready to be revealed in the last time.

1 Peter 1:5

Saints by the power of God are kept
Till full salvation come;
We walk by faith as strangers here
Till Christ shall call us home.

From time to time, President Lincoln expressed concern that the country didn't warrant God's goodness. He worried that the sins of the nation and lack of prayer might cause God to turn against it. In one address he challenged the nation to endeavor to love God and to keep his will. "Let us strive to deserve, as far as mortals may, the continued care of Divine Providence," he said, "trusting that in future national emergencies he will not fail to provide us the instruments of safety and security." Abraham Lincoln was familiar with the Bible and sometimes fashioned his cause to the cause of Moses. Also because he was familiar with the Bible, he knew how God had abandoned Israel when it failed to keep his commandments. Do you warrant God's goodness? Do you worry that God might not be on your side? Keep a pure heart and pray, for God gives safety to those who love him and keep his commandments.

Stay Calm

He that loveth father or mother more than me is not worthy of me: and he that loveth son or daughter more than me is not worthy of me.

Matthew 10:37

Whom have I on earth below?
Thee, and only thee, I know:
Whom have I in heaven but thee?
Thou art all in all to me.

One of Abraham Lincoln's unique characteristics was grace under pressure. He almost always stayed calm. He was able to collect his thoughts, even in times of great stress and as people confronted him. As the tempers of those around him flared, he refused to let his passions get the best of him. Once when anger turned into rage during a cabinet meeting, Lincoln stood calm and self-assured and said, "I appreciate your desire to keep down excitement; and I too promise to 'keep cool' under all circumstances." Lincoln believed that passions ignited bad decisions. They clouded the thought process, caused people to say things they didn't intend, and had the potential to break relationships. He resisted the urge to say a cross word, sometimes even dismissing himself from a meeting and writing his thoughts on paper. Promise to "keep cool," and you'll find that, like Lincoln, you'll never have to regret saying a cross word.

God Gives Strength

For as many as are led by the Spirit of God, they are the sons of God.

Romans 8:14

> *Lead us to holiness — the road*
> *That we must take to dwell with God:*
> *Lead us to Christ — the living way,*
> *Nor let us from his pastures stray:*
> *Lead us to God — our final rest,*
> *In his enjoyment to be blest:*
> *Lead us to heaven — the seat of bliss,*
> *Where pleasure in perfection is.*

Day after day, night after night, Lincoln led the country through the Civil War. The accompanying stress must have been a heavy burden. The knowledge that he might not survive must have weakened his spirits. On more than one occasion, he alluded to his impending doom and death. Where does one go under those circumstances? "I feel that, under God, in the strength of the arms and wisdom of the heads of these masses, after all, must be my support," said Lincoln. It was under God and in the strength of God's people that Lincoln found the support he needed to persevere. It was in the knowledge of God's lasting love and indomitable will that Lincoln placed his confidence. Only because Lincoln believed so strongly that God's will would prevail could he maintain his strength and ability to lead the nation.

Be Guided by Your Principles

Love not the world, neither the things that are in the world.
If any man love the world, the love of the Father is not in him.

1 John 2:15

Why should our poor enjoyments here
Be thought so pleasant and so dear,
And tempt our hearts astray?
Our brightest joys are fading fast,
The longest life will soon be past;
And if we go to heaven at last,
We need not wish to stay.

Lincoln believed that in order to achieve victory, America must put first things first. He believed the foremost priority of the United States was to stay on track morally, to be true to its abiding and original cause of freedom, justice, and equality. He felt that America was to be guided by those principles and that everything ought to follow that moral compass. "If we do not allow ourselves to be allured from the strict path of our duty by such a device as shifting our ground and throwing us into the rear of a leader which denies our first principle, then the future of the Republican cause is safe, and victory is assured." What's your guide? Do you have a moral compass, or do you go through life aimlessly on shifting sand? Only those people who have a moral compass are able to withstand life's tests. Like Lincoln, don't allow yourself to be lured away.

Look at the Heart

They that are after the flesh do mind the things of the flesh; but they that are after the Spirit the things of the Spirit.

Romans 8:5

Let worldly minds the world pursue,
It has no charms for me;
Once I admired its trifles too,
But grace has set me free.

Lincoln was often called upon to make life-and-death decisions during the Civil War. As commander in chief, he had to sign-off on every court martial and on every imprisonment and execution of captured Confederate soldiers. What kind of judge did Lincoln make? Once when deciding whether to imprison a group of men accused of defrauding the federal government, Lincoln had little evidence to go on. All he had were accusations and finger-pointing. So he looked instead at the moral character of the men. "In the absence of a more adequate motive than the evidence discloses, I am wholly unable to believe in the existence of criminal or fraudulent intent on the part of the men of such well-established good character," he finally decided. These men bore good fruit, and without further evidence, he had no reason to believe they could do otherwise. If you follow Lincoln's lead, you will not be quick to judge any man or woman who leads a life of integrity.

God Gives Confidence

Our conversation is in heaven; from whence also we look for the Saviour, the Lord Jesus Christ.

Philippians 3:20

Beyond the bounds of time and space
Look forward to that heavenly place,
The saints' secure abode;
On faith's strong eagle pinion rise,
And force your passage to the skies,
Strong in the strength of God.

When Abraham Lincoln declared the end of the Civil War, he proclaimed that in the United States of America all men are created equal. And he did so by invoking the name of God. "The human heart is with us; God is with us," he decreed. "We shall again be able not to declare that 'all states as states are equal,' nor yet that 'all citizens as citizens are equal,' but to renew the broader, better declaration, including both these and much more, that 'all men are created equal.'" Throughout the Civil War, Lincoln had called on the name of the Lord. He had repeatedly told America to hold fast, because God wouldn't forsake them. And God didn't. At last Lincoln had the evidence he'd been looking for. The country was free, the Union was safe, and all men were created equal. God gave Lincoln confidence. Then he had the evidence.

God Compensates for Lack

The love of Christ constraineth us; because we thus judge, that if one died for all, then we're all dead: and that he died for all, that they which live should not henceforth live unto themselves, but unto him which died for them, and rose again.

2 Corinthians 5:14–15

Be all my heart, be all my days,
Devoted to thy single praise;
And let my glad obedience prove
How much I owe, how much I love.

While some of Lincoln's generals were preoccupied with practical matters of training, weaponry, and war plans, Lincoln sometimes took a more philosophical, or spiritual, approach to the war effort. It wasn't that he didn't care for other matters. Indeed, he was involved at every level. But he cared too for the spiritual strength of his soldiers. Once when a general confided to the president that some of the Union troops were underfunded and may not be ready for battle, Lincoln said, "Whatever shall be sincerely, and in God's name, devised for the good of the soldier and seaman in their hard spheres of duty, can scarcely fail to be blessed." Lincoln had full confidence that God would compensate for any lack on the part of his troops. Do you lack anything? Call on the name of the Lord, and he will compensate for your lack.

Don't Straddle the Fence

We are of God: he that knoweth God heareth us; he that is not of God heareth not us. Hereby know we the spirit of truth, and the spirit of error.

1 John 4:6

Order my footsteps by thy word,
And make my heart sincere;
Let sin have no dominion, Lord,
But keep my conscience clear.

There were a lot of fence-straddlers before the Civil War ensued. People hadn't made up their minds about many issues, particularly slavery. As president, Abraham Lincoln began to warn those who were still holding out. The unity of the nation and the freedom and equality of all people were matters of principle. And principles are not something that can be straddled. "We must remember that he who is not for us is against us," he said, "and he that gathereth not with us, scattereth." Lincoln's pronouncement was reminiscent of the apostle Paul when he wrote to the Romans, "If God be for us, who can be against us?" There is a lot of moral fence-straddling going on these days. Let's ask ourselves whether we are with God. If not, then according to Lincoln, we're against him.

Don't Take Them for Granted

They went out from us, but they were not of us; for if they had been of us, they would no doubt have continued with us: but they went out, that they might be made manifest that they were not all of us.

1 John 2:19

> *When any turn from Zion's way,*
> *(Alas, what numbers do!)*
> *Methinks I hear my Saviour say,*
> *Wilt thou forsake me too?*

While Union soldiers on the front lines succeeded in pushing back Confederate troops all the way to Richmond, Virginia, Lincoln's generals rejoiced. Victory seemed certain, only a matter of time. One night in the Oval Office, President Lincoln reminded his generals not to forget those who gave up the most. "Nor must those whose harder part gives us the cause of rejoicing be overlooked. Their honors must not be parceled out with others," he said. It was true that the efforts of all men and women in the Union helped to win the war. But Lincoln was careful not to take for granted the sacrifices made on the front lines. Whom do you take for granted?

Use Sound Reasoning

Hereby we know that we are of the truth, and shall assure our hearts before him. . . . Beloved, if our heart condemn us not, then have we confidence toward God.

1 John 3:19, 21

How happy are the new-born race,
Partakers of adopting grace!
How pure the bliss they share!
Hid from the world and all its eyes,
Within their hearts the blessing lies,
And conscience feels it there.

What's the secret to Lincoln's success? "Reason," he said. "Cold, calculating, unimpassioned reason must furnish the materials for our future [national] support and defense." Lincoln tried hard not to let his emotions get in the way of himself. He tried to look at situations without giving way to passions that might defer his better judgment. When you make important decisions, do you let reason or emotion drive your motives? Do you sometimes regret the things you do or say in the heat of the moment? Heed Lincoln's advice—use your unimpassioned reason before you take action.

Lean Not on Your Own Understanding

The LORD God is a sun and shield: the LORD will give grace and glory: no good thing will he withhold from them that walk uprightly.

Psalm 84:11

If thou art my shield and my sun,
The night is no darkness to me;
And fast as my moments roll on,
They bring me but nearer to thee.

Lincoln sought hard after God's will concerning the issue of slavery. But the answer didn't come easily. God didn't appear to him in a dream or vision. Lincoln was like most people who seek God's will. He explained, "I hope it will not be irreverent for me to say that if it is probable that God would reveal his will to others on a point so connected with my duty, it might be supposed he would reveal it directly to me; for, unless I am more deceived in myself than I often am, it is my earnest desire to know the will of Providence in this manner. And if I learn what it is, I will do it. These are not, however, the days of miracles, and I suppose it will be granted that I am not to expect a direct revelation." If you're waiting for a miraculous endowment of God's will, maybe you ought to follow Lincoln's lead. Admit that it may not ever come, but continue to believe God will give you an answer.

God Takes Away Fear

All things are yours; whether Paul, or Apollos, or Cephas, or the world, or life, or death, or things present, or things to come; all are yours; and ye are Christ's; and Christ is God's.

1 Corinthians 3:21–23

Let Christ assure me he is mine,
I nothing want beside;
My soul shall at the fountain live,
When all the streams are dried.

President Lincoln once told how God took away his fears concerning the battle at Gettysburg. "In the pinch of the campaign up there at Gettysburg, when everybody seemed panic-stricken and nobody could tell what was going to happen, oppressed by the gravity of our affairs, I went to my room one day and locked the door and got down on my knees before Almighty God and prayed to him mightily for victory at Gettysburg. I told him that this war was his war, and our cause his cause. . . . After that, I don't know how it was, and I cannot explain it, but soon a sweet comfort crept into my soul. The feeling came that God had taken the whole business into his own hands and that things would go right at Gettysburg, and that is why I had no fears about you." Lincoln testified that God took away his fears through prayer.

God Is Sovereign

Blessed be the God and Father of our Lord Jesus Christ, who hath blessed us with all spiritual blessings in heavenly places in Christ.

Ephesians 1:3

Oh the rich depths of love divine!
Of bliss a boundless store!
Dear Saviour, let me call thee mine,
I cannot wish for more.

Sometimes we don't understand why things happen. Despite our earnest prayers and good intentions, things don't always go as we'd want. During the depths of the Civil War, when all seemed lost, Abraham Lincoln reminded the country that God's will always reigns supreme. "We are indeed going through a trial—a fiery trial. In the very responsible position in which I happen to be placed, being a humble instrument in the hands of our heavenly Father, as I am, and as we all are, to work out His great purposes, I have desire that all my works and acts may be according to His will; and that it might be so, I have sought His aid—but if after endeavoring to do my best in the light which He affords me, I find my efforts fail, I must believe that for some purpose unknown to me, He wills it otherwise." When all seems lost, remember that God's purpose reigns supreme. You can trust God.

God Gives Sustenance

In whom we have boldness and access with confidence by the faith of him.

Ephesians 3:12

Come boldly to the throne of grace,
Where Jesus kindly pleads;
Ours cannot be a desperate case
While Jesus intercedes.

Without proper nourishment, the body can't survive. Likewise, without proper spiritual provision, the spirit can't survive. Lincoln struggled to keep his spirit alive during the depths of the Civil War. He readily admitted that without feeding his soul, he would fail. "With my own ability I cannot succeed, without the sustenance of Divine Providence and of this great free, happy, and intelligent people. Without these I cannot hope to succeed; with them, I cannot fail." Spiritual nourishment comes from prayer, from reading and studying God's Word, and from spending time in fellowship with other believers. As the Civil War dragged on, Lincoln reportedly did all these things. He fed his soul with the strength and power of the Lord.

Meditate on God's Word

Elect according to the foreknowledge of God the Father, through sanctification of the Spirit, unto obedience and sprinkling of the blood of Jesus Christ.

1 Peter 1:2

Can aught beneath a power divine
The stubborn will subdue?
'Tis thine, eternal Spirit, thine,
To form our hearts anew.
'Tis thine the passions to recall,
And upwards bid them rise;
And make the scales of error fall
From reason's darkened eyes.

After Lincoln's assassination, two of his top secretaries, Nicolay and Hay, discovered a document Lincoln had written during the Civil War. Lincoln had no intention of making it public, and it was never published. Nicolay and Hay explained, though, that it contained a series of meditations about God in relation to the war. "Wearied with all considerations of the law and the expediency with which he had been struggling for years, he retired within himself and tried to bring some order into his thoughts by rising above the wrangling of men and parties, and pondering the relations of human government and the Divine. . . . It was penned with the awful sincerity of a perfectly honest soul trying to bring itself into closer communion with its Maker," wrote Nicolay. In the midst of chaos and confusion, Lincoln sought to bring a sense of order by meditating on God and his will. Surely that helped to strengthen Lincoln's soul. You too can find peace and tranquility by drawing closer to the Lord.

God Gives a Way

Brethren, I commend you to God, and to the word of his grace, which is able to build you up, and to give you an inheritance among all them which are sanctified.

Acts 20:32

From earth we shall quickly remove,
And mount to our native abode;
The house of our Father above,
The palace of angels and God.

In June 1862 Congressman James F. Wilson brought a delegation to the White House to discuss the conduct of the war and the way it ought to be won. There was considerable concern about the way in which Lincoln was leading the nation in war. Among other things, Lincoln explained to the delegation how God would help find a way. "But I also believe that he will compel us to do right in order that he may do these things," said Lincoln, "and I think he means that we shall do more than we have yet done in furtherance of his plans, and he will open the way for our doing it. I have felt his hand upon me in great trials and submitted to his guidance, and I trust that as he shall further open the way, I will be ready to walk therein, relying on his help and trusting in his goodness and wisdom." Lincoln relied on God to help find a way through the war. As you trust God, he will make a way for you too.

A Vessel of the Almighty

The righteous shall flourish like the palm tree: he shall grow like a cedar in Lebanon. . . . They shall still bring forth fruit in old age; they shall be fat and flourishing.

Psalm 92:12, 14

Lord, one thing we want,
More holiness grant;
For more of thy mind and thy image we pant:
While onward we move
To Canaan above,
Come, fill us with holiness, fill us with love.

Abraham Lincoln considered himself a vessel of God to be used to further the cause of freedom, liberty, and justice. In a letter to the Reverend Byron Sunderland, who called upon the president toward the end of 1862, he wrote, "I hold myself in my present position and with the authority vested in me, as an instrument of Providence. I am conscious every moment that all I am and all I have is subject to the control of a Higher Power and that Power can use me or not use me in any manner and at any time in his wisdom and might as may be pleasing to him." Lincoln was encouraged to know that he was used by God for his purposes. Otherwise, the stress and pressure that came with being president and commander in chief may have been too overwhelming. When one has faith that he or she is being used by God, nothing is too overwhelming.

God as a Source of Strength

Neither yield ye your members as instruments of unrighteousness unto sin: but yield yourselves unto God, as those that are alive from the dead, and your members as instruments of righteousness unto God.

Romans 6:13

Yield to the Lord, with simple heart,
All that thou hast, and all thou art:
Renounce all strength, but strength divine,
And peace shall be forever thine.

Young Henry Rankin was a law clerk in Lincoln's Springfield, Illinois, practice. He and Lincoln reportedly developed a close friendship. Once he asked Lincoln about his belief in the Bible. Lincoln had been going through a tough time and admitted, "I was having serious questionings about some portions of my former implicit faith in the Bible." But Lincoln's troubles seemed to have moved him toward God and a stronger belief in God's Word. "In the midst of these shadows and questionings," he continued to tell Rankin, "... the Scriptures unfolded before me with a deeper and more logical appeal, through these new experiences, than anything else I could find to turn to, or ever before I had found in them." Lincoln's sadness turned to joy as he learned to rely on God's Word. The Bible became a continual source of strength for Lincoln throughout his life from that point on. What is your source for strength? You too can go to God's Word, like Lincoln, and move out of your shadows and questionings.

When You Feel Inadequate

Whosoever therefore shall confess me before men, him will
I confess also before my Father which is in heaven.

Matthew 10:32

> *Should I to gain the world's applause,*
> *Or to escape its harmless frown,*
> *Refuse to countenance thy cause,*
> *And make thy people's lot my own,*
> *What shame would fill me in that day,*
> *When thou thy glory shalt display!*

Lincoln commonly begged the mercy of his friends and colleagues, suggesting that he alone was not worthy of the office
of president. After taking the Oval Office, Lincoln expressed
humility and a certain sense of inadequacy for the task at hand
to Governor Lot Morrill of Maine. But, at the same time, he
said that though he could not do the job, God would assist
him. "I don't know but that God has created some one man
great enough to comprehend the whole of this stupendous crisis and transaction from beginning to end, and endowed him
with sufficient wisdom to manage and direct it."

It's hard to imagine that Abraham Lincoln felt inadequate
for the task, but he felt the same feelings of self-doubt we all
do. How did Lincoln deal with his inadequate feelings? He gave
them up to God. He knew it was when he felt at his worst that
God could work through him. His inadequacy was the very
thing that allowed God to take control. If you feel like you're
not up to the job, don't worry. It's time for God to take over.

Spiritual Reflection

Examine yourselves, whether ye be in the faith; prove your own selves.

2 Corinthians 13:5

> *At evening to myself I say,*
> *My soul, where hast thou glean'd to-day,*
> *Thy labours how bestow'd?*
> *What hast thou rightly said or done?*
> *What grace attain'd, or knowledge won,*
> *In following after God?*

Abraham Lincoln was once criticized for never having joined a particular religious denomination. His critics said he was a "freethinker" and scoffed at the idea of God. On the contrary, Lincoln was more than a freethinker; he was an unabashed man of God. He studied the Bible and spent much time reflecting on his own spiritual walk. Lincoln once said he could not support a man he "knew to be an open enemy of, and scoffer at, religion." Lincoln embraced, not disdained, religion. He followed after God and the things of God. He examined himself and his own heart according to the principles of the Bible. Be a God seeker, even if you don't have a place to worship with others. Lincoln was uncomfortable with church at times but never with God. He took time to pray and reflect. Take time for God.

Contending for the Faith

I . . . exhort you that ye should earnestly contend for the faith
which was once delivered unto the saints.

Jude 3

In the conquests of thy might,
May I loyally delight;
In thy ever-spreading reign,
Triumph as my greatest gain:
Make me conscious by this sign,
Gracious Saviour, I am thine.

For Abraham Lincoln, faith in God didn't come easily.
Maybe that's why he contended so strongly for the faith. Ruth
Painter Randall wrote in her book *Courtship of Mr. Lincoln,*
"It often happens that people who have come through a long,
baffling siege of the spirit, grappling with problems that seem
to have no solution, unable to decide which course of action
to take, cease struggling to turn to their religious faith and
rest their weary souls in waiting for a revelation of divine guidance. Such was Lincoln's state now. He was a man of deep religious feeling. All the rest of his life one finds incidents in which
he placed his reliance on the will of God." Lincoln's faith was
tested by many trials and tribulations, but in the end he rested
his faith in God.

The Body of Christ

We beseech you, brethren, to know them which labour among you, and are over you in the Lord, and admonish you; and to esteem them very highly in love for their work's sake.

1 Thessalonians 5:12–13

How beauteous are their feet,
Who stand on Zion's hill;
Who bring salvation on their tongues,
And words of peace reveal!

Abraham Lincoln believed God's will was made known through the body of believers. "I must trust in that Supreme Being who has never forsaken this favored land, through the instrumentality of this great and intelligent people," he said. "Under all circumstances, trusting to our Maker, and through his wisdom and beneficence, to the great body of our people, we will not despair, not despond." Lincoln relied on God's people to sustain him and the country. He believed the key to knowing God and understanding God's will was through the body of believers.

Salt of the Earth

Ye are the salt of the earth: but if the salt have lost his savour, wherewith shall it be salted? it is thenceforth good for nothing, but to be cast out, and to be trodden under foot of men.

Matthew 5:13

Strive thou with studious care to find
Some good thy hands may do;
Some way to serve and bless mankind,
Console the heart, relieve the mind,
And open comforts new.

When Abraham Lincoln learned of the impending death of a friend's fiancée, he comforted his friend by saying, "I almost feel a presentiment that the Almighty has sent your present affliction expressly for that object. . . . If she is, as you fear, to be destined for an early grave, it is indeed a great consolation to know that she is so well prepared to meet it. Her religion, which you once disliked so much, I will venture you now prize most highly." Lincoln was saying to his friend that there was good in this horrid thing, the death of his fiancée. The good was that he might find God through it. Because of her death, he would become the salt of the earth.

Be a Light

Ye are the light of the world.

Matthew 5:14

Walk in the light—and thine shall be
A path, though stormy, bright;
For God in love shall dwell with thee—
And God himself is light!

Abraham Lincoln took literally the Bible's admonition to be the "light of the world." In a letter, Noah Brooks once wrote of Lincoln, "He said that after he went to the White House, he kept up the habit of daily prayer. Sometimes it was only ten words, but those ten words he had." Lincoln didn't hide his belief in God. He didn't make private his practice to pray and worship God—even in the White House. Lincoln's openness to pray and to believe in God was a light to the nation during the dark days of the Civil War. Through Lincoln's example, the country found the strength to endure. Ultimately, it paved the way for freedom and justice to prevail.

The Reality of God

He which converteth the sinner from the error of his way shall save a soul from death, and shall hide a multitude of sins.

James 5:20

My God, I feel the mournful scene;
My bowels yearn o'er dying men;
And fain my pity would reclaim,
And snatch the firebrands from the flame.

The diary of Secretary of the Navy Gideon Wells gives insight as to how Lincoln ultimately decided to emancipate the slaves. "There were differences in the cabinet, but [Lincoln] had made his own decisions," wrote Wells. But, Lincoln "made a vow, a covenant, that if God gave us the victory in the approaching battle, he would consider it his duty to move forward in the cause of emancipation. . . . God has decided the question in favor of the slaves." According to Wells and others, Lincoln made the decision to free the slaves only after spending time in prayer and making a vow before God. For Lincoln, God was the final court of appeal. He was more than an esoteric ideal; he was a very personal and practical source of power and enlightenment.

God's Gift of Scripture

Render to all their dues: tribute to whom tribute is due; custom to whom custom; fear to whom fear; honour to whom honour.

Romans 13:7

Our sovereign with thy favour bless;
Stablish the throne in righteousness,
Let wisdom hold the helm:
The counsels of our senate guide,
Let justice in our courts preside,
Rule thou, and bless the realm.

A few months after Mary Lincoln joined the First Presbyterian Church in Springfield, Illinois, she persuaded her husband to visit the church with her. Abraham Lincoln reportedly took great interest in giving a session lecture there on the Bible. His lecture centered on the gift of God's Word and how the Bible formed the "moral code" of the nation. "It seems to me," taught Lincoln, "that nothing short of infinite wisdom could by any possibility have devised and given to man this excellent and perfect moral code. It is suited to men in all conditions of life and inculcates all the duties they owe their Creator, to themselves, and to their fellow man." The Bible was Lincoln's primary guide in life. He felt it applied to all of life's conditions, and he leaned on it heavily during the terrible conditions of the Civil War many years later. What's the basis for your moral code?